HEALED

WITH

STYLE & GRACE

BY JAI HUDSON

ISBN 978-0-9966866-0-0 (soft cover)
ISBN 978-0-9966866-2-4 (hard cover)
ISBN 978-0-9966866-1-7 (E-book)
Cre-8ive Publishing
New York, NY 10804
WWW.CRE-8IVEWORLD.COM

JAI HUDSON

CONTENTS
FOREWORD 8
ACKNOWLEDGEMENTS 13

JAI HUDSON

JAI HUDSON

FOREWORD

By Misa Hylton

It is with great honor that I write this Foreword. I have been along for Jai Hudson's journey to the completion of this book, and it has blessed me in a myriad of ways. This book is a work of healing, growth, freedom and passion. Sexual abuse is a sensitive topic for many people and a source of shame for many children who have had to endure it. Jai was one of those children.

I met Jai as a young girl, fresh out of college in the beginning years of pursuing her career in fashion. We met through a mutual friend and just like that Jai became a favorite and an asset to my fashion company, Chyna Doll Enterprises. Jai was fresh out of Syracuse University — super creative, hardworking, trustworthy, a team player and a true gem. It didn't take long to notice that Jai was hiding or hiding something or hiding from something, or maybe all of the above. When Jai became comfortable, she decided to share her secret with me — she had been sexually molested by her stepfather, her younger sister's father.

Jai also said that her mother knew about the molestation and that her mother was still married to this man. At that moment I knew just how special Jai was and that her purpose was much larger than her pain and what she may have thought and felt about her life. We connected through fashion, but the purpose would prove to be far greater.

Over the next 14 years we continued to work together and became family. My family and friends became her family and friends. We circled around her with love and support. I have been with Jai through many ups and downs, many rough days and many rough nights. The torment of the abuse haunted her. She wanted answers that she could not get. She wanted understanding for something not comprehensible. She had become stuck emotionally; even as an adult she yearned for her mother to choose her, and this yearning left her feeling incomplete and abandoned, not important, or as she would say, "invisible." She felt as sick as her secret. This was a feeling that would not leave easily. It spilled into many other areas of her life, sometimes creating a stagnant energy, a cycle of poor relationships, and an overall feeling of sadness. Then one day the breakthrough began. The light found the smallest crack in her beautiful existence, a tiny opening where the healing could start. Grace was given, her healing had begun, she took the first step towards her power — something she had not taken the opportunity to become familiar with before.

This book is a great work, it is a story about a young girl whose childhood was violated, and despite the odds she received grace. God provided her with everything and everyone she needed each moment of her life. She chose to heal, she chose to share her secret with you, she chose to take her experience and use it to help others who have also found themselves in this position, in this dark place, and she offers hope.

It is with my pleasure and blessing that I introduce you to a great work, God's work. As you take the journey with Jai, as a little girl born and raised in Brooklyn through each stage of the abuse and each stage of her life to the passionate and dynamic woman who was Healed with *Style and Grace*.

DEDICATION

JAI HUDSON

When I sat down to write this memoir, it was as if the words just poured onto the pages. My mom said she would help me and she did. I want to dedicate this book to the loving memory of Donna Elcock. My angel, the softest place to fall, my security, my 22, my life giver, my mommy, Donna O. Elcock. 6.22.57 –4.02.14. I love you.

I would also like to dedicate this cre8ion to two women who helped me see myself, a soul who helped me to be myself, and three spirits who renewed me and helped to embrace the new me.

Talia Parkinson, You may have looked at our past as us having a great friendship; I look at it as so much more. I learned love. I learned how to receive it and I am eternally grateful to you. With all my hiding, you saw and accepted the real me. Thank you.

JAI HUDSON

Misa Hylton, You have become a living angel for me. You and your family saved me. Thank you and I appreciate you. You also were part of the push I needed to complete this book. I am grateful to you. My coach, my sister, my bestfriend. I love you.

Walter Steele Jr., my twin soul. You see my soul every day. You are a healer and a selfless Angel who I thank God for every single day. I am thankful we found each other. I love you.

Justin Combs, Niko & Madison Brim, I don't believe in teachers being of a certain age. You all have been amazing teachers for me. Niko you showed me myself. You provided the inspiration I needed to go after what I want. You showed me to stay true to who I am. I thank you for that. Madison, you are an incredible, warm, caring, loving and beautiful spirit. You accept me and I see you. I am so grateful for you. Justin Combs I will forever love you for opening up your huge heart to me. You may not know how much you made me feel comfortable in just being. Thank you from the bottom of my heart to you all. I love you.

Lastly, this creation is dedicated to all the young children who are suffering. I want you to know you are not alone. You are never alone. God is always right by your side guiding you. You may not be able to see him, but I promise you, that day when it seems like the worst ever, don't give up, tomorrow the sun will shine again. To all the women who have been abused or know someone who has dealt with a past of pain, this book is dedicated to you. You are my motivation. *We will overcome!*

JAI HUDSON

REVIEWS

Your story is compelling!!
-Kim Snow

Thank you, Jai, for sharing part of your impressive background and for taking on this highly relevant issue.
-Rod Williams
B.E.S.T. Talent Management Solutions

HEALED WITH STYLE & GRACE

JAI HUDSON

GRACE: "The Love And Mercy Given To Us By God Because God Desires Us To Have It, Not Because Of Anything We Have Done To Earn It."

PREFACE

"To All My People In The Place, With Style And Grace..." –Notorious BIG (Big Poppa)

"AMAZING LOVE"

SONG BY LUTHER VANDROSS

Got to tell you how you thrill me
I'm happy as I can be
You have come and it's changed my whole world
Bye-bye sadness, hello mellow
What a wonderful day

It's so amazing to be loved
I'd follow you to the moon in the sky above
Ooh...ooh...ooh...ooh...ooh...ooh...ooh...ooh..I'd go

And it's so amazing, amazing
I could stay forever, forever
Here in love and no, leave you never
'Cause we've got amazing love

Truly it's so amazing, amazing
Love brought us together, together
I will leave you never and never
I guess we've got amazing love

JAI HUDSON

THURSDAY MARCH 20, 2014

As I entered the Metro North train at Harlem station, I could feel that this would be a ride like no other. My headphones filled my ears and soul with Notorious BIG's *"Big Poppa."* I visually scanned to the left and right of the train to find a seat. I then walked to my right and sat in the first set of four seats to my left. I sat by the window and began to enjoy my 22- minute ride to New Rochelle. Suddenly the song switched to Luther Vandross' "Amazing Love." As I listened to Luther I decided I was going to try to talk to my mother again. "Amazing Love" was our favorite song, so maybe that was the inspiration for my deciding to have this conversation. Something told me to do it now. In the past I always spoke about our unspoken secret in person, but this time I felt like texting. This time I would get all of my feelings out without being interrupted. This time my mom would know how I really felt about the past.

(Exact text messages sent on March 20, 2014)

Me:
Can I ask you a question: Was I important to you? Because I feel like I wasn't good enough or important enough for you to choose me instead of choosing your husband, knowing the things he did to me. I have lived my whole life never feeling worthy or good enough. This is really the last hurdle for me so I can be free from the past.

Mom:

You are always important to me and worthy too. I never chose anybody. You are my daughter and I love you.

Me:

I didn't come first because you allowed me to endure that pain. Because you didn't make him leave; as a child I took that as meaning I wasn't important. He abused me (still brings tears to my eyes). He robbed me of natural growth and the ability to love a man free from judgment. I just need to know — why?

Mom:

I'm sorry for all your pain. As I said before I didn't choose a man over my child!

In the past, a statement like that usually caused me to "back off" and retreat, and I think my mom knew this about me. She usually said something that would make me discontinue the uncomfortable conversation. But if I were to truly get over this, I had to try something different. So no, I wasn't going to back down this time. I picked up my phone and continued to text.

Me:

Did you stop being with your husband? Did he remain in the house? Do you understand that's why I left home? You made *me* choose. That's a lot for a child. I'm very strong and I would go thru fire for you because you're my mom and I love you deeply. But did you ever think about me? How I felt? I have to get this out because it has been holding me back so much by not expressing my deep feelings to you.

Mom:

JAI HUDSON

If I can change what happened to you I would. I do not want you to hurt. You are my first-born. I miss not hearing from you or seeing you. I wish I could turn back and save my little girl. I hurt for you very much. I do love you very much.

At that moment, my soul was at rest. I wanted her to acknowledge my pain and for her to truly hear me. And she did.

So I replied:
I forgive you.

Mom:
I'm glad you forgive me. Can we move on and regain our mother and daughter relationship? I really want us to be close again. I really miss you.

I felt so free from the heaviness I had been carrying around from not fully expressing to my mom how the abuse affected me. There were so many fears that kept me from something so simple. I am so grateful that I followed my intuition that day to communicate with my mom. Something I kept trapped inside for so many years had now not only been freed in me, but also released from my mom. Forgiveness is freeing.

That was the last time I spoke to my mother. Four days later she went into cardiac arrest. That was the last time I would share how I felt about our little secret.

As you read this book and hear my words, you will enter my world. A world where as an adult I thought I had it all together. I was living my dream as a fashion stylist, developing music acts, and living a life I viewed as a blessing. However, I continuously had moments of darkness, which I usually allowed my mother to help me through. But now she was gone. I was carrying our secret all alone. No one truly understood me enough to even start to help me. The person who knew my pain and unconditionally loved me was no longer physically here. She was no longer here to say what I needed to mask the darkness. I had to do it on my own.

INTRODUCTION

JAI HUDSON

What does this all mean? Why am I here? Why do I experience these recurring periods of depression? Why do I not love myself the way I see others love themselves? Why can't I forgive myself? Why do I continuously experience this déjà vu in my romantic relationships? Why do I constantly doubt myself? Why do I still feel this pain? These thoughts and feelings constantly filled my head. No matter how much I tried to cover it up or hide from it, these feelings always resurfaced.

The past seems to do that. As much as I tried to run from it and not deal with it, it came back harder and with more vengeance. I was 33 years old and still having these recurring experiences where that situation I had not dealt with internally kept resurfacing. It was like I couldn't move to the next level emotionally. I believe that God shows us lessons in the form of opposition. Those really tough situations we go through are our greatest teachers. I also believe relationships are our greatest mirrors for self. We learn who we are, we learn healthy and non-healthy emotions, and we learn what makes us happy.

My past had abuse in it, and no I did not deal with it. I tried desperately to move on and force myself to be OK. However, it kept reappearing, showing up in my romantic relationships, friendships, work, how I dealt with people, and my emotional stability. At first I couldn't recognize the situations as extensions of my past. I thought it was just normal experiences, your typical drama. I couldn't see why I kept having the same types of romantic relationships, or why I always ran from situations that required a certain level of intimacy. I was paying my dues and working hard, but couldn't see that I was afraid to shine. In the beginning of my healing, I couldn't see that feeling not good enough or able to experience greatness was all connected to my past. All of these situational triggers stemmed from something really basic: feeling like I wasn't "good enough."

My life situations constantly brought me back to the same place. It was a never-ending cycle. I'd think I was doing OK for a while, and then something would happen. I felt stuck, like something was in my way, preventing me from accelerating. I didn't want to feel this way anymore. So I had to figure out why I couldn't move forward and what was truly in my way. What was the roadblock? Why did I keep feeling this same old way, year after year, situation after situation, time after time?

After a long period of looking deep within myself I realized the opposition that stood eye-to-eye with me all these years, was *me*.

JAI HUDSON

I had been standing in my way. I could blame others for my hardships, but realistically no one was to blame at all. Realizing this, and truly accepting it, was huge! I didn't want to accept the fact that it was me; it was easier to keep blaming others for my stagnant behavior.

I had to emotionally deal with my past so that I could finally move on, once and for good. Finally forgive myself. Learn to love others and myself in a healthy way.

I thought I loved myself enough.
I thought I knew my power.
I thought I was confident.
I thought I trusted myself.
I thought I was truthful with myself.
I thought I had dealt with the deep emotions inside.

JAI HUDSON

I thought wrong. I didn't — couldn't — love myself enough to heal, until this realization. I decided to put an end to the recurring scary dream. Heal that six-year-old little girl inside from a life of abuse, so that adult Jai could move on, and live a purposeful life.

"AINT NO HALF STEPPIN"

Song by Big Daddy Kane

Another victory

They can't get with me

So pick a BC date cause you're history

I'm the authentic poet to get lyrical

For you to beat me, it's gonna take a miracle

And, stepping to me, yo that's the wrong move

So what you on, Hobbs, dope or dog food?

Competition I just devour

Like a pit bull against a Chihuahua

Cause when it comes to being dope, hot damn

I got it good, now let me tell you who I am

The B-I-G D-A-double D-Y K-A-N-E

Dramatic, Asiatic, not like many

I'm different, so don't compare me to another

Cause they can't hang, word to the mother

"CHA CHA CHA"

Song by MC Lyte

I'm the dopest female that you've

heard thus far

and I do get better, the voice gets wetter

nobody gets hurt (as long as you let her)

do my thing with an '89 swing

the dopeness I write, I guarantee delight

to the hip-hop maniac, the uptown brainiac

in full effect, mc Lyte is back

and better than before as if that was possible

my competition, you'll find them in the hospital

visiting time, I think it's on a Sunday

but notice they only get one day to shine

the rest of the week is mine

and I'll blind you with the science that the others have

yet to find

so come along and I'll lead you the right way

just clap your hands to the words I say, come on...

JAI HUDSON

BROOKLYN BRED

Growing up in Brooklyn NY — Bedford
Stuyvesant, to be exact — was a great
experience. I like to say I was born in
Brooklyn and raised in Harlem. My 20- block
radius was like its own microcosm, filled with
block parties, music blasting from cars,
burning wax for skelly tops, the smell of
cook-outs from the neighborhood parks,
Albee square mall, kids playing outside,
knock-knock zoom-zoom, sidewalks filled
with chalk outlining hopscotch games,
champion jackets, fights over Jansport
strings and Jordan's, running home from the
midget league basketball games, the
performances at the basketball games,
rapping on my stoop with Jay Hitch, double-
dutch tournaments, dancing contests, blimps
writing in the sky… the music! There was so

JAI HUDSON

much culture. I had a lot of freedom to dream big — and a whole world to explore.

MUSIC IS MY WORLD

Optimism ruled my world as a child. I had a thirst for information — always dreaming and eager to learn something new about something new. My mother tried to show me a picture of hope. A lot of the kids from my neighborhood really didn't leave the neighborhood; I'm not sure if it was fear or contentment. Some families grow comfortable with a situation or environment, and change just seems too grand. However, my mother was different when it came to my experiencing the world outside of Bed Stuy. I was very creative and passionate growing up, and my mother supported my talents. I was involved in a lot of extracurricular activities. I wrote stories and music, I was in a singing group, I danced, I played basketball, and I also did a few commercials. But music has always been my first love. That was my escape. The place I could be invisible. In music I felt like I could disappear from everyone and everything, and be in my own world.

Music was a place I could be free and stop time. Words resonated with me. If my feelings had a sound, the words and melodies of music would describe them perfectly. Take Diana Ross' "Do You Know?," or Jackson 5's "Ben," or even Quincy Jones' "We Are the World." As a child, these songs and music as a whole, were magical.

Because of my connection to music, I decided to start each chapter of this book with a song that would bring you to a special place and time in my life. These lyrics inspired me and became a companion on my journey to healing. I am so thankful for music because with all the experiences, the bad and the good, music has the ability to touch the innocence within. Because of music, I always knew my life would be better. I always had something to look forward to. Music has the power to save lives, it universally connects different races across the world, and it expresses love. That's powerful.

So, to fast-forward for the moment through my life, I would say I was a happy child. I had reached certain goals I had set for myself. I got good grades. I was respectful. I worked hard. I have even travelled the world for work, seeing parts of the world I had only imagined. My eyes have seen so many beautiful things.

However, in the 1980s there was also a lot of poverty, drugs, and violence. Ronald Reagan was president and the crack epidemic was at an all-time high. I remember visions of small clear vials with red tops lying in the staircases and in the cracks on the sidewalks. Back then I didn't know what they were, but I saw them everywhere in my neighborhood in Brooklyn. Poverty, drugs, and violence were all connected. Homelessness, crack and shootouts were normal things to the kids in my neighborhood. Culture, art, and music took us away from all of this. I escaped all the harsh realities by dreaming. However, growing up in the "hood" you learn to cope with whatever is thrown your way. It's how we survive. That's true everywhere. We all have the ability to adapt to our surroundings and adjust. However, our environment calls us to build up these walls of protection. Some call it "thick skin," or dealing with reality.

I found myself going through life creating invisible shields, protecting myself from

being hurt, not only from my surroundings.
You see, I had been hurt by someone.
Someone I was supposed to be able to trust.
At first, the shields I had put up were tools of
protection. However, after "the threat"
disappeared I continued to hold on to these
shields and found I got further and further
away from what was truly real and important.
In other words, I had built up strong walls of
defense but there was no longer a reason to
defend myself because my life had changed.
In my teens I built them up against my peers
and parents. Then in my 20s I was still in
constant shield mode and started to protect
myself heavily in love and in work. When I
reached my 30s the same shields from my
teen years didn't work anymore. I was
reacting to present situations with the same
emotions from childhood. My protection
mechanisms no longer served a purpose,
not to mention it no longer felt good. I didn't

want to defend myself anymore. I mean, who was I shielding from anyway?

I wanted to feel better but I didn't want to deal with the thing that caused my sadness. Or why I suffered from depression. It was just too painful. It was like opening a can of worms, not really knowing what was inside. I feared dealing with my feelings about my abuse. But not dealing with them was preventing me from truly moving forward, from being free. I had to stop resisting and just "go with the flow."

In the midst of all the wonderful experiences, great relationships, and friendships, that recurring feeling always seemed to slip through. I started to pay attention to myself and look at why I kept having the same feelings over and over. What was I going through when these feelings resurfaced? When I stopped for a moment within this fast-paced world and truly thought about it, I realized it was my past disguising itself as Love. It kept showing up as periods of depression, or it would show up as sadness within my relationships. It was like I was afraid of something. Like I kept running away from something. In my mind it was easier to forget the past. I mean, I was functioning, I was working, had great relationships, and people loved me.

However, It was like clockwork. When my emotions were pushed into an uncomfortable place, the past came back. I knew I had to accept the truth that this was directly related to the relationship with my mom and a past full of pain. The pain was all about my feelings about my abuse.

In daily life I realized I was either anxious (over-thinking future plans) or depressed (over-thinking the past). Rarely was I living in the moment. Always preparing for my future

but at the same time running from the past. I
have gone through life facing my challenges,
experiencing new things, falling in love,
learning and growing, becoming more
spiritual, and living life. In the midst of all this
I was still avoiding the core. A pain that I had
experienced affected me more than I
acknowledged. I needed to heal. I had to
finally deal with all the things I was hiding
and running away from. I needed to heal the
inner child that was abused.

INTENTION

My intention is to tell my story and free
myself of all that I kept hidden. All I had been
running away from. All that I wanted to make
disappear in my mind. I want to face me. I
know that I learned a lot through this
experience. Through my experiences,
reading some incredible books, seeking
answers, listening to some of the most

amazing teachers, being soothed by melodies and the beauty of music, and facing my truth. I have now healed a part of me that was broken for a long time. My intention is to share my healing story through the words written on these pages.

Healing resides within your experiences and your perceptions. The antidote to any pain is viewing it differently. Young people, women, or anyone who has experienced some form of sexual abuse or abuse in general — all require healing. Abuse is more common than you may think. I believe there's someone who has been abused in everyone's life. So many of my friends have been abused and still hold on to their pain in the same way I did. They may feel they have moved on, but after hearing my story they will be able to decide if they have truly faced the abuse.

JAI HUDSON

From the first act, the person violated is affected. It's like falling into quicksand. With each violation you fall deeper and deeper. As a child suffering from sexual abuse, this experience can cause a child to withdraw from the world. Slowly the child's innocence begins to fade and the ability to value themself diminishes. I speak from personal experience. My mother's husband, my younger sister's father, sexually abused me from the age of 6 to13 years old.

I remember the first time the abuse happened, I remember feeling alone and the self-love meter began its trickle downward. Even though the abuse happened so long ago, there seemed to be this shadow standing in front of me, not allowing me to excel in my adult life. I felt stuck. No matter how much I tried to pretend, there was an anger deep inside for the person who abused me and I continuously blamed my mother for allowing me to endure that pain. I felt these feelings towards my mother because she didn't do enough to protect me. Although I told her each time I was violated, she stayed with him. She argued with him a little, he left for a couple days, but he always ended up back in our home. And it didn't stop. I know it sounds crazy, right? My mom stayed with him even after I told her I was being sexually abused. This is deep, and sadly I am not the only person who has this story.

Through my story, I have made sense of the residue left behind. All the blame, pain, and anger I carried within. I no longer wanted to feel stuck. I wanted the recurrences to stop, or at least not to trigger the same reactions. I needed to accept all of me. I decided I wanted to live more in the present. My past would no longer control me.

JAI HUDSON

It was extremely difficult at first to shed myself of a truth that may have no longer been as accurate as it has been in the past. I had a perspective that was *my* viewpoint and shaped from a past of trauma. I wasn't being violated anymore, so why did I hold up the same shields? I was so angry and couldn't see how I could start to forgive. I didn't want to see pain differently; therefore, I didn't see the pain differently.

However, I was healing and I didn't even know it. It was happening just by my wanting to feel differently. When the routine or ride became too redundant, I wanted off. That's the first step in healing: realization that you want something better. My goal was to free myself of this cycle and that's what I was focused on. So the healing began as soon as I faced myself.

I believe that one of the reasons why many of us don't feel balanced and headed toward our soul purpose is because we are afraid of it. We tend to become trapped in the constant motion of this practical world. This *hamster wheel* doesn't have time for the unpredictability of our creative imagination. We are distracted by our problems, worries, and memories from the past, or fears about the future. We have stopped dreaming. We abandoned the idea of exploring who we truly are and what we deeply desire. The moment we can let go and trust in the Universe, God, the higher power, Source, we will experience freedom and complete living in the moment. The answers are there and just because we cannot see the path, the guidance is available always. We can then discover our passions and purpose in life. Releasing the past creates new life.

I know you will relate to something you hear. If you walk away feeling differently about something you have been dealing with in your life, then I have accomplished my purpose in sharing my story. By you receiving this book, it confirms that you are on the road to Victory! Open your heart and mind. And focus on *you*.

If you thought about *your life* as a *movie* you were directing, the **plot** is the **abuse, the challenges and recurrences.** The **climax** is the **survival, the healing,** *and releasing* yourself of a *painful past.* Let's make this an Oscar winning movie. Our lives are just that special. So let's make it good!

PART I
MY STORY

JAI HUDSON

"MY LIFE"

Song By Mary J. Blige

If you looked in my life and see what I've seen...if you
looked in my life and see what I've seen...if you
looked in my lifeand see what I've seen...if you looked
in my lifeand see what I've seen...

Life can be only what you make it
When you're feelin down
You should never fake it
Say what's on your mind
And you'll find in time
That all the negative energy
it would all cease

And you'll be at peace with yourself
You won't really need no one else
except for the man up above
Because he'll give you love

JAI HUDSON

ENDLESS LOVE

I learned to forgive on March 20, 2014. It was a major challenge to get to this place, but let me back up and explain how I got here.

"Endless Love" by Diana Ross has always been my favorite song. My mother gave me my favorite song when she introduced me to Diana Ross and the Supremes. That song has always connected with me so deeply. Who knew that my mom was really singing this to me?

I remember being 4 years old and hearing that Diana Ross was coming to NYC. I couldn't believe it. Yes, I was only 4 years old. I begged my mom, and of course she got us tickets. I loved Diana Ross. Everything about her was just so amazing to me — 1983, Central Park, "Endless Love"?

JAI HUDSON

There was no way in the world I could miss this.

You know that feeling of being a kid and being excited about going somewhere? You can't sleep the night before because you're so excited? That was me. Nothing could ruin this amazing experience. I even cleaned up my toys, was extra pleasant, and had my outfit and sneakers ready for the next day. I was ready! However, as it has happened a million times before, it *rained on my parade*. Yes it rained. It was a heavy storm too. I just knew Diana was going to cancel. There was so much talk about Diana in NY. So much excitement that she couldn't cancel. But the storm was serious. Still, she showed up.

I learned something that day. Even in the pouring rain, she could not disappoint her fans. She wouldn't disappoint her fans. She cared. Even in the rain, she showed up. Wow! Anyway, my mom told me that it wasn't safe to go in the rain especially for a 4 year old. I was crushed. It felt like the world was ending. I guess my tantrums worked because at the last minute she decided we were going to go. I don't remember arriving at Central Park, nor do I remember specific details. All I remember is seeing Diana Ross in her red catsuit performing "Ain't No Mountain High Enough" in the pouring rain. She performed like it was 80 degrees. Her performance was so amazing and I was with the person who introduced me to music —my mom.

CREATION

On the 22nd of May of the year 1979 on a Wednesday I, Jacquetta Nadesha Elcock was born to the world. Yes, growing up I hated my full name. No one could ever pronounce it correctly. And because my last name had a specific word within, it became total embarrassment whenever I was asked my name. I always wished for a simple name like Erica or Michelle. However, my mother named me after my great-grandmother Isma Jacquetta King.

"Mama King" was what we all called her — you could tell what she was like just by her name. Everyone knew Mama King. She was a light brown- skin toned woman with silver hair. She was very slim yet strong and sassy. She let her opinion be heard, always. She was the head of the household when I was born. She took care of everyone. She was such an amazing woman to be named after.

I grew up in building 1865 of Brevoort projects in Bedford Stuyvesant, Brooklyn, Apartment 5A. I grew up around my uncles and cousins, my mother's best friends Debra and Ronnie, and a whole lot of children in the projects. My mother got pregnant at the age of 22. She was attending Hunter College and decided to leave school to care for me. She also had a job at HPD (Housing and Preservation Development).

She hid her pregnancy from my great grandmother for as long as she could. At 11:22 on May 22nd I was bought into the world by Donna Elcock and Richard "Ricky" Washington. I heard I was a pleasant child. She had a smooth labor and pregnancy. I heard that at a very young age, I had a mind of my own. I was outspoken, talented and smart. I was a dreamer.

My mom was my first experience of pure love with no conditions. The first person to tell me "I love you." The first person who loved me unconditionally — my introduction into the world. We shared a bond that is indescribable. I guess that's the mother-child connection. But ours was different. From the first day I can remember, I wanted to protect her. I don't know what or who I wanted to protect her from, but that's how I felt. That might sound crazy because it should be the other way around, seeing as she was the mother. Still, I had strong feelings regarding protection, healing, and my mother, deep in my soul. At that age I just didn't know what those feelings were about.

DONNA

My mother, Donna Olga Elcock, was born June 22, 1957 in Brooklyn NY. She grew up in building 310 and moved to 1865 Fulton Street at the age of 10 when my grandfather passed. My mother never really talked about her mother. Grandma passed when my mom was 16. Her name was Elouise "Owweee" Elcock. I heard she had an aggressive personality and drank a lot. "Owweee" regularly threw parties in the house, inviting people from the projects and neighborhood. I never had the chance to know my grandma but my great-grandmother Mama King filled that void, and I considered her to be like my grandma. She hated taking pictures so it was really difficult to find any good ones of her.

My mom lived with Mama King and her five brothers. She had a sister that passed away when she was about 11 years old. I heard a few stories about her. Her name was Deniece. She was disabled and never learned how to walk or even function as a child. I heard that she screamed curse words regularly, and because she never learned to walk, her legs dangled in front of her. She dragged herself across the room using her hands. My family kept her hidden and didn't let anyone see her. I also learned that they never took her to the doctor to find out what was wrong or to see if her condition was permanent. That told me a lot about my family back then. She was a secret in the family. I don't know if it was embarrassment but it seems like it was tradition to keep family secrets. But I always wondered, would she have lived longer if she were treated?

Lorenzo was the oldest of my mother's five brothers: he was an accountant and also the spitting image of my mom. He passed away when I was about 3 or 4 years old. A vein busted in his head and he died instantly. Georgie is the comedian of the family. He moved away before I was born, so I hardly saw Georgie. Daryl was on drugs. He stayed in the house also, I remember he'd steal valuables to support his habit. I remember he stole my gold name ring when I was young. Dwayne was the youngest and heavily into the fast life of selling drugs and gang life. He always bought me the latest clothing and sneakers. And then there was St Clair, my favorite uncle. He was the smartest man I knew. And he cared about my feelings. We connected on a level I could never put into words. It was the way he made me feel… I loved him so much. He passed when I was 12 years old from AIDS. I'm not sure if he ever knew what he was to me. He championed my excitement and even though he was a grown up, he made me feel like an equal. He tutored me whenever I needed help, he listened to my dreams, and he championed me just for being me. I sure do miss him.

My mother's father, Lorenzo Elcock, passed when my mom was a preteen. My mother, great-grandmother Mama King, and my uncles raised me. Mama King was born in Barbados and her accent never left her even after spending so much time in New York City. Everyone in the projects said I resembled Mama King. They said I walked like her, I had an attitude like her, and spoke

up like her. I didn't understand at the time
but I sure do now.

She protected me. That's the beauty of
grandmothers. You are instantly considered
their *baby*. Mama King gave me two black
and white scarfs when I was young. Every
night before school my mother did my hair
so she wouldn't have to do it before going to
work the next morning. That was her system
she developed so we would have smooth
mornings. However, I loved playing with my
hair because it helped me fall asleep. So
when I woke up the next morning, my hair
was a mess. My mother was not happy.
When my mother wasn't happy she spoke in
a high-pitched voice and arched her bushy
eyebrows. I did my best to avoid this
reaction.

So Mama King came up with a solution to
the problem. She found a way for my hair to
remain neat without compromising my sleep

aids. She tied a zebra printed scarf on my head and told me to wear it every night. She also gave me a black scarf with gray circles as a backup. I wore it every night. Eventually during the night, the scarf ended up in my hands. The texture of the scarf felt so good in my hands. Because I now had the scarf to help me sleep, I no longer messed up my hair. Problem solved. That was Mama King — she always had the answer. I still have one of the scarfs to this day. It became my protection for the night time. Thank you Mama King for always protecting me and being my gift of *Grace.*

My mom was about 5 feet tall ,with a very light skin complexion. They used to call her *"ole yella."* She had the bushiest eyebrows ever and *chinky* eyes. My mom loved playing handball. She was on her high school team. She attended South Shore high school in Brooklyn NY. My mom had three best friends growing up. Debra, Ronnie, and Ann. Debra and Ronnie were sisters who lived on the 7th floor and Ann lived right below us on the 4th floor. Debra and Ann became my godmothers.

Debra told me a story of when she first met my mother. My mom moved to #1865 when she was about 11 years old. She used to live in another building on the other side of the projects with her mother. When my grandmother passed, my mother moved into Mama King's apt in 1865. My mom was extremely shy. All the kids played in front of the building. Because of this, my mother ran in and out of the building to avoid the attention of the kids. Crowds made my mother nervous. She felt like it was *all eyes on her* and that kind of attention made her uncomfortable.

So she ran past the kids out front every time she entered and exited the building.

JAI HUDSON

Debra noticed this and couldn't understand why my mom never stopped to say hi. So one day Debra and Ronnie were outside playing when they saw my mom about to make her regular exit out of the building. They went over to the door and caught my mom before she began her usual 100-meter dash. Debra asked, "What's your name?" "Donna," my mother responded. Debra then introduced herself and her sister Ronnie and told her she didn't have to run past them anymore. Debra then invited her to play.

My mom was very quiet but had a smile that would light up a room. She also loved to laugh. She was the type of person that would help you if you needed her. A lot of people depended on my mom. She took care of her brothers when her mother died and also took care of Mama King, as she got older.

JAI HUDSON

YOUR EYES TELL ME HOW MUCH YOU CARE

Eyes are the windows to the soul. They basically tell your story. As a kid, I didn't know this. I did know that different eyes created a different feeling within. My mother's eyes said a lot. They displayed an abundance of love, a genuine care, and a hidden pain. I could see this, even being as young as I was. I would say I saw a pain that was definitely disguised as strength. My mother was an "honorable" type of person. She handled her responsibilities and was a major support system for many. I noticed this and that was partly why I wanted to protect her and show her love as much as possible. I wanted her to be happy, and for the most part she was.

My mom and I were extremely connected. It's weird, because it felt so cosmic. I was chosen to be her child for some apparent

reason. It's hard to explain but I truly feel this in my heart. Back when I was younger we were so different, and my mom constantly pointed out our differences. She was very quiet and shy, and I was talkative and outspoken. My mother always made it clear I was different. It was like the qualities she lacked I had, and vice versa. That's why I feel like I was her child for a reason.
Growing up, I didn't know that being different was a good thing. After hearing about all my differences, which seemed like all the time, I wanted to change who I was — I guess because back then I wanted to be just like my mother. Everyone depended on her and loved her, and she was just an overall nice person. I admired that. I wanted to grow up and be someone everyone liked as well. God makes no mistakes; my mom and I had a close connection and I was who I was for a reason.

JAI HUDSON

RICKY WASHINGTON

One night my mom decided to go out with one of her best friends, Carol-Ann McCoy, to a nightclub. This is when she met my father: Ricky Washington, a tall dark and handsome man from Linden Houses in Brooklyn New York. Ricky was very intelligent and loved fashion. My father worked as an accountant, but he would get his suits and clothing custom-made and tailored.

I would say I never really knew my dad. I mean, he came around when I was younger. But there are a lot of qualities inside and outside that I believe I got from him. Like, my eyes, my height, my fascination with numbers, my fashion sense, my mannerisms, my face… I remember he'd come over to great-grandma Mama King's house in the Brevoort projects. The memories are vague but if I close my eyes I can remember seeing him walking through

JAI HUDSON

the door. My father was about 6 feet, slim build, brown-skin complexion, striking eyes with long eyelashes, and he was always dressed to impress.

When I heard he was coming I would run under the long wooden and metal table in the kitchen to hide. I was afraid of him. Those striking eyes of his were so scary to me. When he arrived, I remember hearing his voice call out for me to come out of hiding. His voice was so distinct. I knew it was him. All I saw from under the table was dark blue jeans and some high top Nike sneakers. I loved sneakers, even at that age. I think my father started my obsession with sneakers. Then he reached his hand under the table for me to come up from under the table. I grabbed his hand and he'd whisk me up in his arms and hug me so tight. When I looked into his piercing eyes, it was like I was looking at myself.

JAI HUDSON

This became the routine when my father visited me. I also remember what it felt like seeing my father. He loved me. I could tell that just from being in his presence. I heard he loved my mother so much also. I was very young, around 2 or 3 years old, so observation was how I learned. I always wondered why my mom was never there when he came to see me. I didn't understand what was going on between my mother and father at that time.

I overheard my mom and others talk about him. It was usually negative things that caused fear within me. But I didn't know him. I'd hear, "*He's selfish; he's trying to kidnap you,*" and "*Jacquetta, you look just like your father.*" How could I have good feelings toward him after hearing these things over and over? Not to mention that his piercing eyes looked super scary to me as a child. My family said a lot of things that made him seem like the big bad wolf to me. And my mother was never there when he came to see me. So all of these things created *not-so-good* emotions about my father. Back then I didn't know that was only one side of the story — only half the truth.

My father loved my mom. My father loved me. I never knew why my mom broke up with him. From what I remember, one day everything was all good and the next day it wasn't. I remember one day I went to Coney Island amusement park in Brooklyn NY with my godmother Ann. I loved Coney Island. Even though I never liked roller coasters, I loved to play games, eat Nathan's Fried Shrimp, and ride the bumper cars. As we walked through the park, I saw all the bigger kids standing in line to ride the famous cyclone rollercoaster, and the super popular Himalaya ride. I always loved to walk near this ride because they played the latest music. This ride was a circular train that rode over a track with hills on the path. The Himalaya went round and round to the latest hip-hop and R&B hits. Then it went backwards and everyone cheered. It was so cool.

We decided to walk on the boardwalk overlooking the beach. As we did, I saw my godmother's mood change. Then she became anxious, saying that we had to find a pay phone. At this time there were no cell phones, beepers, nothing mobile. We found a pay phone and Ann made her call. She turned her back to me as she spoke, but of course I could hear bits and pieces of her conversation because Ann spoke very loud. I overheard her say, "He's here. I'm coming back." After she hung up she picked me up and we walked swiftly toward the exit. Suddenly I saw who all the commotion was about. Why we were rushing out of Coney

Island. Who she was talking about when she said *he's here*. It was my father. He stared at me from a distance as Ann carried me away. Did he follow us? How did he know we were there? It was like a scene from the movies. This scene happened a few times. So that became a routine also. He'd show up in places I was and I would be rushed away. I wonder if my mother saw him lurking as well? I was always told that my father was going to kidnap me. I never fully understood what that meant. Why would my father need to kidnap me?

This routine happened for a while, until my mom met a new guy. From my perspective and the stories I heard, I've come to this conclusion. I heard my dad was super jealous and thought that sneakers and clothes were more important than diapers and formula. I also heard my uncles didn't get along with him. He was also heavily in the streets and clubs, which didn't go along with my mom's plans at all. It was also told to me that he started to change and he became paranoid and aggressive.

I went from seeing my mother and father together happy, to weekly visits from my dad with Mama King chaperoning. Then I was told he wanted to kidnap me. I started to fear him. Then he disappeared. I can only imagine how hard it was for my mom to get away from my father. I heard he would come to Brevoort projects and just sit in the "circle playground" looking up at our apartment window. He wanted to be near us. He wanted to be near my mom. He couldn't understand why he was losing his world. I trusted my mom, so if she thought it was best to not be around my father then I was OK without him.

Then it was just my mother and I against the world. She'd take me everywhere. I loved

her so much. I felt so safe. I always knew I
would be OK. I could see that my mother
held everything together. She was the glue.
She made everyone feel so safe. I can still
feel what it felt like being hugged, kissed,
and praised by my mom. It was such a great
feeling that energized my soul and made me
feel invincible. She saw me and heard me. It
was the feeling of unconditional love. My
mom was my hero.

THICK SKIN

My mom rarely expressed her own feelings,
although she was very nurturing and
affectionate when I was very young. I hardly
ever saw her cry. She never had to
physically discipline me either. She had the
power to give me a certain look and from
that look I knew right from wrong. There
were only two times I've ever seen my mom
cry. One time was when I was about four or

five years old. I was being my usual self, talkative and active. My great aunt was babysitting me when I said something that pissed her off. When my mother returned home from work my aunt immediately started to tell my mom what I did. I rushed into my room to figure out what I was going to say in response. I knew my mom was headed straight to my room once my aunt finished telling on me. When my mother came in, she gave me "the look."

Her arched bushy eyebrows basically said it all — my mom was not happy. She began scolding me in her high-pitched voice. I always just listened when I was being scolded. But for some insane reason, I responded with a statement that I would never forget. I don't know what I was thinking. I must have been a little crazy. I usually blame it on being an outspoken

JAI HUDSON

Gemini. However, I said to her, "That's why your mother is dead and mine isn't."

I don't know what I was thinking. I don't even know if I was thinking at all. Why did I say something like that? I must have been crazy for real. Looking back I can see that I was attempting to help my mother face her emotions but, back then I just thought I was a little cuckoo; a crazy Gemini. She responded with a stare that seemed to pause time.

Everything stopped and a tear slowly dropped from her eye. It was followed by a continuous flow of tears. My mother was crying. I said something that caused her pain. I remember thinking to myself that I never wanted to do that again. Something I said caused her pain. My first lesson on how words hurt. She didn't say anything. I told her I was sorry and we never spoke of it again. My mother had tough skin, but what I said opened a door to a world of pain that I never wanted to unlock again. I wanted my mom to be proud of me. I loved her so much and wanted to be close to her. I wanted her to be happy.

country

One cold night, I remember going to Juniors —*"home of the best cheesecake"* — located downtown Brooklyn. I was about three or four years old, but I remember this day like it was yesterday. My mother wanted to introduce me and my cousin Wendy to a guy she was seeing. Henry "country" Green was a cook at Junior's Restaurant. I remember when I was introduced to him I did not get good vibes. It was *not* "like at first sight." I didn't know why but the gut never lies. It was like a tight sharp feeling in my stomach. I just knew I didn't like him. I wasn't the type of child that didn't like people when first meeting them. I was a friendly child and very smart for my age. But for some reason with country, I just knew I didn't like him. I forced myself internally to give it a try because my mom liked this guy. I had never seen my mother excited in this way.

country was a very weird guy. He was a mason, drove sports cars, shot a lot of people, got robbed every Friday, and a Brooklyn's ladies man-*let him tell it.* He was also *the valedictorian of pathological liars.* This man lied about everything. If someone was a pilot, country was an astronaut. It was unbelievable. Watching him lie to my mother almost every payday about being robbed for his paycheck was so hurtful, but also valuable information about the kind of person he was, if we could only see it. My mother accepted his lies and I always wondered — did she really believe him or just accepted him, flaws and all?

JAI HUDSON

I always tried to understand how my mother must have felt. She got away from my father. Then she met a guy who was the total opposite of my father. He wasn't stylish like my father. He *was* attentive to my mother and he said that he wanted to adopt me. He also wanted to marry her. Dating country also kept my father away. Maybe she felt like she struck gold. Whatever she felt, my mother had emotional holes left from her childhood, and somehow country must have filled her needs. It was a very confusing time for me because I knew who my daddy was, but it was like my mother wanted country to father me.

That feeling I felt back then about country, I now recognize as intuition. *Yes I know*, most children don't get along with their step-parents. I've heard all the horror stories about having a stepfather from my friends. However, this was not the case with me. I just intuitively felt negative energy about him.

Mom and country got married May 6, 1984. That was a very sad day for me. I remember I did not feel well and even woke up with pink eye that morning. What were the chances of my getting pink eye on the morning of their wedding? I got an A for effort, but of course it didn't stop anything — the wedding must go on! Right? Yes, it most certainly did and I still had to perform my duties as the flower girl. I was not a happy camper. When I heard the pastor say, "If there is anyone who objects to this union, speak now or forever hold your peace." I thought to myself that this was my time to speak up — as I remembered from the movies. I thought I had to do something to stop country from becoming "my father." But then I thought about how my mother would feel. There was no way I could do that to her on her wedding day. I stayed away from her that day. I allowed her to have her day without my feelings regarding country ruining the day.

SHOWDOWN

I remember one day after school as I waited with my classmates Roslyn Smallwood and Talisha Martin, I saw familiar eyes approach me and say "Hi." It was my father. He came to my school to see me. I guess he felt this was the only way to see me without other family members interfering. He spoke with me and my friends for a short while, until my teacher came over and escorted me to the office. I didn't know that my teachers and school had been alerted that if my dad came they were instructed to get me away fast. I was so confused. I didn't know why my mother wanted to keep me away from my father. I didn't feel he was dangerous and if he wanted to kidnap me, wouldn't he have done it already?

I don't know how country found out my dad was at my school. When Mama King came to pick me up from school, I saw my dad and country fighting in the middle of the street on Patchen Avenue. I was terrified. I saw my father walking away swiftly. Then I saw country start to chase him. My father picked up a metal garbage can and threw it at country and hit him. Mama King and I saw what was happening from the next block, however she grabbed my hand tighter and rushed me home. On the inside I was happy to see my father hit country with that garbage can. I know that is not a nice thing to say. So God please forgive me.

JAI HUDSON

"IF YOU SAY MY EYES ARE BEAUTIFUL"
Song by Whitney Houston

If you say my eyes are beautiful

It's because they're looking at you

And If you could only see yourself

You'd feel the same way too

You could say that I'm a dreamer

Cause I had a dream come true

If you say my eyes are beautiful

It's because they're looking at you

MY CARDS DEALT

When country moved into our room in 1865 Fulton St. apt 5A, I remember he tried to adopt me. However, Mama King wasn't going for that and I'm so glad. She was very vocal, especially because my mom might have done it otherwise. I don't think Mama King cared for country much either. When he wanted to adopt me I thought on one hand that someone wanted to be a father to me, which felt kind of good. And since I trusted my mom and she loved this man, maybe I should want this too. But on the other hand, It just didn't feel right. Even back then, my intuition was strong. My feelings were telling me things, but at that age I had no way of knowing what those feelings meant. It was truly a blessing that my great-grandmother was there in the house. She was a protective voice for me during that time —one of my many gifts of Grace.

JAI HUDSON

LEOTTA SELENA GREEN

My mom said I could give my baby sister Leotta her middle name. Leotta was named after Mama King's twin sister. So I thought hard about what middle name I would choose. In my elementary school, PS 21, a friend of mine had just lost her mother. I remember that was the first time I dealt with the death of a parent. She was so sad; I remember after the funeral she never came back to school. I was so sad for her. I couldn't imagine what that could felt like. My friend's name was Selena.

On August 26, 1985, my baby sister was born: Leotta Selena Green. I was six years old. Leotta was born prematurely and the doctors didn't think she would live very long. The image of my sister, less than a pound in weight, with several tubes coming out of her teeny body in an incubator, will never disappear from my memory. My mother had two miscarriages before my sister was born. When my mother's water broke at six months while pregnant with Leotta, she had to have a C-section. I think my mother and stepfather really wanted to have a child.

country married my mother and moved us out of the housing projects. We moved to 276 Bainbridge Ave, actually right across the street from Brevoort. I wanted my mother to be happy, however I still wasn't having happy feelings about country.

I loved my younger sister and I loved being an older sister. I loved dressing her like me, styling her hair, and we would play for hours in our bunkbed tent. My sister had a few life-threatening scares early on in life. When she was two years old she was in a major car accident. One day, my uncle Darryl picked up my sister from Pacific Day Care Center. Usually, my Uncle Dwayne or St Clair would pick up Leotta from daycare.

JAI HUDSON

However, they both couldn't do it this day, so my Uncle Darryl went instead. When they reached the corner of Atlantic and Ralph Avenues, a car jumped onto the curb and hit my sister, sending her two-year-old body flying up in the air. She landed on the pavement on her face. My uncle was hit from the impact of the car hitting my sister. He suffered a broken arm.

I remember I was home with my stepfather when he received the call that my sister was in an accident. He was cooking dinner as usual; I remember he had a ham in the oven. When he received the news he rushed out of the house, forgetting the ham that was still baking. Soon after, my Uncle St Clair came by and took me to meet my mother at the train station. We walked over two blocks to Utica Avenue A train station. My mother had been on the train coming home from work when my stepfather received the news. So my uncle and I went to meet her at the train station to tell her what happened.

When we saw my mother exit the Utica Ave train station, my uncle and I rushed over to greet her. He told her what happened and I watched my mother's face go from surprise to instant worry. She ran over to the curb and hailed a cab. As we drove down Atlantic Ave towards Kings County Hospital, we passed the corner of the accident. I quickly peeked out the window to see if I would see any trace of the accident. And I did. I saw one of my sister's pink power rangers sneakers on the ground. I knew then it was real. I also kept thinking about the ham that was in the oven still cooking. I thought to myself, would the house burn down? Would there be a fire when we got back home? I never said anything about the ham to anyone though. I think I secretly wanted the

JAI HUDSON

house to burn down, I really disliked that house.

When we got to the hospital, they told my mom that my sister had stopped breathing. However, they were able to revive her. I just remember hearing that she was gone. But somehow she pushed through. Everything was happening so fast. *My sister died but came back to life?* I didn't understand what this all meant. I kept hearing that the car hit my sister and *she fell flat on her face.* I couldn't imagine what that looked like. Then they said her jaw was completely broken. They had to put a brace in her mouth. I was eight years old and hearing these things terrified me. I was afraid to see my sister, so I waited awhile before going into the hospital room to see her. Leotta spent a month in the hospital.

When we got home that evening, the ham that country was cooking had burned completely. There was no fire. But I will never forget the smell it created within the house. That scent lingered on in the house for quite a while. Sometimes I smell that same scent, and it brings me back to that day.

Because Leotta was only two years old, she had to relearn the simple things like walking and talking again. My sister is a fighter and even at two years old she beat the odds. It was like she was reborn.

The second thing that happened to my sister was when she was in middle and high school she suffered from seizures. Some so strong we almost lost her again. The doctors and neurologist said that the seizures were a result of the accident. They prescribed her a seizure medicine and told her she needed to take the medicine her entire life. My sister is an Angel. She is definitely a miracle.

JAI HUDSON

So I only vaguely remember this short
time that followed, but I will try my hardest to
recall. I blocked out certain moments in life;
that's how I protected myself, I guess.
Certain memories were just too painful.

276 Bainbridge St. was a cream with
burgundy-trimmed brick brownstone. The
brownstone was a three-family house. We
lived on the 2nd floor in a railroad type
apartment. country's uncle owned the
brownstone. A short dark-skinned named
Guy lived in the basement and a couple lived
upstairs. I really disliked this house. It had a
dark energy.

However, I did like my friends that I
gained on Bainbridge. I spent a lot of time
across the street with my friend Haj Chinzera
Pinnock. Her parents were African and were
super loving and cool. Her mother was a
movie director and her dad was an actor. I
remember being home watching TV and the

movie *Who's that Girl* with Madonna came on. Haj's dad, Mr. Pinnock, was the cab driver driving Madonna. This was the first time I saw someone I knew in a movie. I was so amazed and intrigued. I learned a lot from Haj. I celebrated Kwanzaa, learned to build tents, went to museums and Broadway plays, and most importantly, learned that it was okay to be myself, no matter what. Thank you Haj.

Sometimes I'd hang out on my stoop with my friends Jamel Hubbard, Charles Dupass, and Shamoneek. Most of my friends on Bainbridge Street had parents in their households, unlike the projects, where it seemed to be populated with single moms supported by other family members. I started to live two separate lives: I had my friends Niesha, Naquan and Jay from Brevoort and then I had my friends from Bainbridge. The two worlds were so different. Most of my friends had stepfather's they didn't like very much, so my feelings toward country seemed normal.

22

TRUST YOURSELF

"EXPRESS YOURSELF"

Song by Salt-N-Pepa

You know life is all about expression

You only live once and you're not coming back

So express yourself, express yourself you gotta be

you

Express yourself you gotta be you and only you babe

Express yourself

Let me be me

Express yourself

Don't tell me what I cannot do baby,

Come on and work your body.

MY CULTURE, OUR CULTURE

Although I moved across the street from Brevoort, I developed a system for how I spent my time between both places. I'd spend all day in the projects and return to Bainbridge early in the evening. I also had a curfew that I had to be on my block by 9pm. I had fun in Brevoort and all my family lived there. But now I lived on Bainbridge St. I remember details of my past through different senses — like smells, pictures, and sounds. The smell of hot dogs immediately brings me *back to the late 80's Albee Square Mall on Fulton Street — the hotdog shop. I remember eating hotdogs and drinking pina colada drinks with my mom. I also remember a lot through music. During this time Kid n Play's "Getting Funky" and "Aint Gonna Hurt Nobody" was huge. Do you remember MC Lyte's "Cha Cha Cha?" Salt-N- Pepa's*

JAI HUDSON

"Push it?" BDP's "Self Destruction?" Or
when Public Enemy shut down BedStuy with
the "Fight the Power" movement? This was
the music I was listening to at this time.
Music felt so good and expressed different
messages, whether it was Black power, safe
sex, or simply having a good time. Music
was used to project a message globally.
Young artists were expressing themselves
and it was reaching the masses. These
events were happening within the streets of
New York City. Even if you're too young to
know this music, you can YouTube it and still
get the feeling.

I loved to dance, sing, and rhyme. I
continuously wrote music and created dance
routines, preparing myself for my big break. I
knew it would happen, too. I competed in
every competition at my school PS 21 with
my god-brother and performance partner
Naquan. He is Debra's (my godmother)

youngest son. He was a year younger than me. It was like we were twins. We were attached at the hip. We were always creating and dreaming bigger than big. Debra created our matching costumes and helped us get our performances together. We were both shy but we came alive on stage.

Naquan and I did everything together. I remember we'd hang out in Brevoort all day. We played basketball, baseball, created dances — we did it all. I remember walking to the Ralph Avenue side to Carvel to get orange sherbet ice cream, a mini pint of pork fried rice and duck sauce from the Chinese restaurant, and a 35-cent Sunnydale pina colada juice drink. That was my favorite snack. This was my culture.

Growing up in Brooklyn New York during these times, kids learn survival and a way of life. There's a culture within every block and in my case every housing community. We had certain games we played like skelly, hopscotch, knock knock zoom zoom, red light green light, hot peas and butter, 7 11, dancing contests, double-dutch, playing 7up in school when there was a substitute teacher, break dancing and back flipping, slap boxing, mother may I, creating cheers to perform, doing the kid n play dances, etc. If you grew up in the hood then you know about this, you may have called it something else, but the culture is so universal. We didn't have cell phones. We had walkie-talkies and made listening devices using cups and strings. We built clubhouses and used our imagination. Those cardboard houses were our mansions and the cars that rode by were our newest rides. We would watch cars pass for hours, each trying to beat the next person to call out "my car." We dreamed.

JAI HUDSON

Culture was so fresh and organic. It came straight from the soul. That's how it felt. We were creative and believed anything was possible. The style was through the roof also. *Colorful 8 ball and triple fat goose jackets, rope chains, gumbies and flat top haircuts with tails in the back, asymmetrical hairstyles, kufi caps, gold and African inspired medallions, high top Air Forces, Bo Jackson and Patrick Ewing sneakers, Dwayne Wayne flip glasses, door knocker earrings, gold caps, Shearling and sheep skin coats, my favorite penny loafers with dimes in the hole instead of pennies, shoulder pads, Nike track suits, graffiti,* and so much more. The late 80s and early 90s was a great time for style. We were being creative with no restrictions. Hip-hop music was also solidifying its pedestal within music.

My mother saw that I had a strong sense of individuality, and that being creative and expression was a major part of it. She had a carefree attitude. She went with the flow. Whatever I wanted to do she found a way for me to do it, but wasn't vocal about it. She would surprise me by finding a way to do what I wanted to do. She loved to surprise me. That told me that she was listening to me. That meant a lot.

Christmas with my mother was amazing. She did fun things to continue my belief in certain things — like the tooth fairy, Santa, and the excitement of Christmas. She wanted me to believe in the beauty of things like that. She always said, once you don't believe anymore the thrill is gone.

So I believed for as long as I could.

JAI HUDSON

III

MY ABUSE

"LEAN ON ME"

Song by Kirk Franklin, Mary J Blige, Jewel, Bono, R. Kelly

And There's A Girl
Searching For A Father And A Friend
Praying That The Storm Someday Will End
But Instead Of Walking Away
Open Up Your Heart And Say

I Am Here
You Don't Have To Worry I Can See....Your Tears
I'll Be There In A Hurry When You Call
Friends Are There To Catch You When You Fall
Here's My Shoulder, You Can Lean On Me

"THE SECRET"

I looked to my mother for guidance. She was the only person I trusted with all my heart. She protected me from my father. She made me feel OK being different. She showed me all things were possible. I know now it was tough raising a daughter without the proper tools. I applaud your fight. I love you… you were, and still are, my hero.

My name is Jai Hudson (formally known as Jacquetta Elcock) and I was molested/sexually abused by my mother's husband —my sister's father, country. This is actually the first time I wrote these words and actually said them inside. It's so freeing. I assumed it would feel victimizing to say it aloud or even to write it. I never wanted to use abuse as a crutch.

The first time the abuse happened I was asleep in my room that I shared with my

younger sister. We lived at 276 Bainbridge
St. The apartment was railroad style. There
were two ways to get in and out of my
apartment. Think of a railroad train. When
you entered the house, the first "railroad car"
was the bathroom, followed by the kitchen,
then my mother's bedroom, connected to my
sister and my bedroom, followed by the
living room. Each room is like a railroad car;
you have to go through one room to get to
the next. You could enter through a door
near the bathroom or the living room. I really
disliked railroad apartments.

country walked around the house
inappropriately. He'd wear loose bikini brief
underwear, exposing the silhouette of his
private area. It made me feel very
uncomfortable. *I guess he thought he was
sexy.* During this time I really enjoyed
watching WWF wrestling. *Ultimate Warrior*
was my favorite wrestler. I loved his flashy

costumes and the dances he did when he entered the ring and when he did an exciting wrestling move. country knew this and tried his hardest to connect with me. He'd call me into his room to watch wrestling on the bigger TV. I never wanted to go but I did. I tried to give country a chance. I usually sat at the edge of the bed, very uncomfortable. Once I forgot where I was and became relaxed watching the wrestling show, I became less uncomfortable. *I guess that was country's cue.* country suddenly tackled me re-enacting a wrestling move from the TV show. I hated this. It made me feel sick in my stomach being touched by him. He made it a habit to have his private area touch me or brush up against *mines.......* I hated this! My mom was never there for this and my sister was very young. I made him stop and usually ran into my room. I had to find a way to get this all to stop.

JAI HUDSON

The first night it all happened was like every other night before school. I always looked over at my sister to make sure she was asleep before falling asleep myself. After falling asleep, it felt like maybe a few hours had passed when I suddenly felt the covers lift off my body. I was still asleep but somewhat coherent to my surroundings. Next, I felt my pajama pants start to slide down from my waist to my hips. Was I dreaming? I wasn't a deep sleeper at all. I mean, there are definitely times when my sleep is deeper than regular, but this was not one of those times.

I kept my eyes closed and continued to think that it must be a dream. Then suddenly, when my pajamas reached a low enough place, I felt a hand began to touch me. I felt someone's hand searching for my private area. This was not a dream. I quickly opened my eyes because the feeling felt too real. All I could see was a male figure run into the living room adjacent to my room. I wiped the sleep out of my eyes so that I could focus my sight on the person running from my room but I couldn't see clearly. It was too blurry. Who was that? I felt so weird. I was confused. The shadow running away was a familiar silhouette. I kept thinking, *"Why did this happen?"* So many things ran through my head.

My cousin James was staying with us at that time. He was a very hyper child. I overheard the family say he had ADHD. His mother was mentally challenged and his grandmother, my great-aunt was too old to give the attention James needed. So my mom insisted James stay with us. My mother tried to care for him, however country took over, as always. I witnessed some really mean things.

James attended PS 21 with me. We were in the same grade. Whenever a teacher called the house saying James was disruptive, country had to teach him a lesson. My stepfather closed the sliding doors to the living room. He'd tell James to get naked. A few seconds following, I'd hear the whooping sounds of a tree branch being raised in the air and then popping James' skin. Every time it hit his skin I'd hear him cry. After what seemed like hours of torture, my stepfather opened the sliding doors and made an alcohol bath for James to sit in. How painful was that? My cousin endured this every time country received a negative report. I started to think that was the way boys were disciplined.

After seeing the male figure run away that night, I remember thinking, "Was it James?" I mean, we were so close, a year away in age, so I thought maybe it could

have been him. It seemed a little more
normal with children around the same ages.
I immediately got up and went into my
mom's room. I thought about following the
figure, but something stopped me and I went
straight to my mother instead. I think I was a
little afraid to see who it was.

　　When I entered her bedroom, I saw that
my stepfather was not in the bed with her. I
didn't hesitate telling my mother at all,
because I knew she would make it better. I
told her "someone touched me the wrong
way in my sleep." I told her I didn't see who it
was. She was still half-asleep, but looked
like she recognized something. It was a
puzzled look. She immediately got up and
went toward the bathroom. I went in the
other direction back to my room. I lay on my
bed in the dark, and thought about what just
happened. It was different than the times a
male cousin tried to touch me while sleeping.

JAI HUDSON

It felt different. Even though I didn't see who it was that touched me, deep in my heart I knew who it was. My mother then came in and sat next to me. She touched my face and asked me if I was OK. I said yes, and closed my eyes. She stayed with me until I fell asleep.

Walking to school that morning was super weird. I couldn't get what happened out of my mind. I was so confused. I kept telling myself it was my younger cousin being nasty. I couldn't understand why this was happening. I knew that this would change my life forever. I thought about my mother and what she might have felt that day. I was so scared because that feeling was not a good feeling at all. I was young and didn't know how to process what had just happened. I immediately thought it was my fault. Something I was doing must have created this type of situation to happen. I thought maybe I was being punished.

I was in 2nd grade at PS 21 and I remember feeling so unfocused in class that day. I couldn't get what happened out of my head. I kept having these flashbacks of what it felt like on and in my vagina. It felt weird and embarrassing at the same time. I also kept trying to tell myself it was my cousin, but deep inside I knew who it was. I guess I thought it wouldn't happen again, maybe the person felt I caught them, maybe they made a mistake, and maybe because I told my mother she would take care of it.

THE ROUTINE

The next time it happened, it was a similar type of evening. The only difference is the fact that it had happened before. This second time it happened was long after the first time. He waited until it was a distant thought and our guards were down again. In the middle of the night as I slept, I felt the breeze from my bed covers being raised again. Then my pants slid down slowly and a hand reached into my underpants. However, I woke up at the right time to see who it was. My sight was super clear and I was now staring straight into the eyes of the person who was guilty of violating me. It was him, my mother's husband, my sister's father, country. I felt so violated. The look in his eyes is a look I will never forget.

He frantically gave an excuse for why he was under my covers and attempting to get my pants off. Something about me "kicking the blanket off me and it's cold, blah blah, blah." It was all gibberish to me because I felt him lift the blanket off me. I didn't know this at that moment but this would be a life-changing situation.

Again I rushed into my mother's room and told her "country touched me." The look on my mother's face was priceless. She seemed to be saying in her mind, *Why is he doing this?* Looking back, I know that her expression was more like, *Why is he doing this again?* The energy she gave off was like she knew this could happen. Maybe she saw the signs? Deep, right?

But what did this all mean? Why was my mom's husband touching me the wrong way? Was this normal? Was I supposed to continuously experience this? This was super confusing.

The next morning I walked to school and felt so different. It was like I was in a bubble. That's how I physically felt. Nothing looked the same out of my eyes. Nothing sounded the same. I didn't even feel the same. I felt like "The Boy In The Bubble." (An old-school movie about a boy who had a disease and

couldn't live outside of this plastic bubble.)
He couldn't receive and experience love
physically. He couldn't be a normal kid. No
one understood how he felt because they
weren't inside of his bubble. That's how I felt.
I felt disgusting and dirty. The person my
mother was married to was doing things that
didn't feel good to me. What should I do?
Should I tell my teacher?

But then I thought, my mother knows, so
I should be fine. Right? Hmmm. I just didn't
know what to do. Hopefully, it wouldn't
happen again. Maybe that whole thing didn't
even happen at all. Maybe I was dreaming.
So many thoughts filled my head. I hated
what was happening to me. I hated what he
was doing to me.

I didn't know how to trust myself or my
intuition I was experiencing. That feeling I
felt when I first met country was real to me
and now I knew why I felt that way. That was

my first connection to something super-
natural like God. I say this because the
feeling was super strong and didn't feel like
something to be ignored.

What was happening to me didn't feel
good. I tried so hard to prevent him from
abusing me. That may sound a little crazy,
but I figured if I could tuck my sheets and
blankets tightly around me and wear several
layers of clothing to sleep he would give up
or I would wake up before he got to me.
Sometimes he got into my underwear. I'd
wake up to find one of his hands in my pants
touching my private area and the other hand
rubbing my chest. But sometimes he didn't
get the chance to get that far. Something
would wake me in enough time to catch him.
This became my routine for bedtime. I
developed a system. I also prayed to God
that it wouldn't happen that night. "Please
God, don't let him touch me tonight." Then I

thought about the best plan to keep him away. I tried several things to make it difficult for him.

My mother knew what he was doing-I told her every single time. Every night became a routine of preparing for the possibility of him doing it again. If it wasn't going to stop, then I had to do something to prevent it from happening. He was a coward anyway. He waited till I fell asleep. He couldn't manipulate me like he did with others. Not saying I wanted that, but when I think about how he treated me, it most resembles fear. If I accomplished something great, he had to one-up me to my mother. It was like he was in competition with me. *Yes, competing against a 6-year-old female who he wanted to adopt and father.* I also thought he probably was mad because I didn't want him to adopt me. Or did he think adopting me would make it easier to abuse me? country

JAI HUDSON

knew that he would never have that control he wanted over me. Of course I didn't know this, or couldn't process things this way back then, but I do know that now.

I'm so thankful it didn't go as far as penetration with his private parts — at least I don't remember that. I am so thankful. He had excuses every time I caught him abusing me. Some of the most famous ones were: #1. "Your blanket fell off of you and it's cold;" #2. "I was looking for the remote to turn down the TV;" and #3, the most commonly used excuse given by country was (drum roll please), "It was a mouse in the room." He should receive an award for the dumbest excuses ever!

He was very crafty. Everyone liked him. He had the gift of gab-master manipulator. But every time he violated me I ran into my mother's room and told her what just happened. A routine developed. He violated me, I immediately told my mom and she'd get up and address him. She usually found him somewhere in the house acting as if he was doing something super important that time of the night. But most importantly he was not in the bed where he should have been. The routine ended each time with them arguing, followed by the slam of the door. It went sort of like this:

Mom: "Why are you touching her?"

country: "I am not touching that girl."

Mom: "Why are you even in her room?"

(Excuses on top of excuses given by him)

country: "I ain't taking this shit; I'm out of here."

Immediately following, country would put on his clothes and leave the house. When he was gone I felt better, but the energy of the house had changed forever. It became a waiting game. My mother wanted him to return, and my sister couldn't understand why her father wasn't home. I had a few days to relax but I usually spent that time awaiting his return too, but for different reasons. So I really didn't get a chance to relax. That was also the time I used to prepare for the routine.

A few days later he'd come back home. He'd wait two or three more days and then start it all over again. Around this time I developed eczema. Eczema is a skin disorder that creates dry patches on your skin. I developed discolored spots all over my legs. I looked like a Dalmatian. I didn't know why this was all happening to me. I used to think I caught eczema from a couch at Mama King's house that my Uncle Darryl used to sleep on. Back then my cousins and I called the sofa in the living room the "*cooty couch.*" My mother took me to several dermatologists, but they all said the same thing — it was something I was allergic to. Back then we didn't have Google so if we wanted to find out symptoms we looked in an encyclopedia.

It was the same abuse routine from the time I was six to about thirteen years old. He violated me, I told my mother, he left for a couple days, and then he'd return. My mom even instructed him to put a lock on my door to keep him out. Yes, the same door that was connected to my mother's room. However the living room was the other way to get to my room. There was no lock on that door. He installed the lock, which means he had the key. So even with the lock, he always found a way in. Did she think a lock could really stop him?

I continued to wear several layers of clothing to sleep and still tucked myself in tightly within my comforters and prayed he

JAI HUDSON

would give up or I'd wake up in time. I hated
myself. I started to think it was my fault. I
hated that I had to feel like this. I started to
think that if I hid physically under baggy
clothes and made sure I wasn't "pretty," he
would stop. I hated him touching me and
looking at me the way I saw him look at
grown women. I witnessed him flirting with
other women like my godmother Ann, and
other random women. I didn't understand
why was he was doing this to me.

One time during "the routines" I was
faced with the ultimate decision. So, it
happened same as usual. He violated me, I
told my mother, and he left.... But this time
he may have been gone longer than before
—four or five days, instead of two or three.
Picture this, my sister in the corner crying..."I
want my daddy." My mother was clearly
unhappy. She wanted her husband to come
back home. My mom asked me, "What do

you want me to do? Do you want me to tell him not to come back?" This was the first time I made the decision to put someone else's feelings before mine. Something that would affect my happiness and steal my joy for a very long time. I basically put myself last and chose to endure molestation and pain so that my sister could have her father and my mother could have her husband.

But what about me? I was only about ten or eleven years old and experiencing such a tremendous burden. Wow, on the one hand, did I really have that much power? On the other hand, I saw my sister in pain because she wanted her dad. Then I saw my mother frustrated and wanting her husband to return. Those emotions from my mom and sister took precedence over my feelings.

So...I told my mom he could come back.

JAI HUDSON

"WATERFALLS"

Song by TLC

I seen rainbow yesterday
But too many storms have come and gone
Leavin' a trace of not on God-given ray
Is it because my life is ten shades of gray
I pray all ten fade away seldom praise him for the
sunny days
And like his promise is true
Only my faith can undo
The many chances I blew
To bring my life to anew
clear blue and unconditional skieshave dried the tears
from
My eyes no more lonely cries
My only bleedin' hopeis
For the folk who can't cope
Wit such an endurin' pain
That it keeps 'em in
The pourin' rain who's to blame
for tootin' caine in your
Own vein what a shame
You shoot and aim for
Someone else's brain
You claim the insane
And name this day in time
for falling prey to crime I say the system got you
victim to your own mind
Dreams are hopeless aspirations in hopes of comin'
true believe in yourself the rest is up to me and you

JAI HUDSON

IV
THE AFTERMATH

JAI HUDSON

"TELL HIM"

Song by Lauryn Hill

Now I may have faith
To make mountains fall
But if I lack love then I am nothin' at all
I can give away everything I possess
But left without love
Then I have no happiness
I know I'm imperfect (I know I'm imperfect)
And not without sin (and not without sin)
But now that I'm older
All childish things end
And tell him...
Tell him I need him (yeah)
Tell him I love him (tell him)
And it'll be alright
[background singing] tell him be alright be alright
Tell him tell him I need him
Tell him I love him
It'll be alright
Now I may have wisdom
And knowledge on earth
But if I speak wrong then what is it worth?
See what we now know is nothing compared
To the love that was shown when our lives were
spared

JAI HUDSON

HUSH

After making the decision to allow him to come back I was told to keep this to myself. *No one should know about our family secret.* Writing this hurts my soul so much, because it always felt like I chose the abuse. Not only did I feel like I chose it, but I felt so unworthy and not good enough to be protected. I wasn't worthy of my mother's protection and security. I felt so low and confused. I didn't want to talk anymore. My words caused so many issues within my family. That was how I felt. I didn't realize that because my mom asked me what I wanted, that was really saying she didn't know what to do. And that question was the time for me to say I didn't want the abuse. I didn't know what to do either.

Being faced with a decision like this at such a young age weighed tremendously on me. I didn't know how to express what I truly wanted and have it be parallel with what my mom and my sister wanted as well. Because what I wanted was something they did not want. What I truly wanted would change our lives forever. What I really wanted was for him to disappear forever.

101 DALMATIONS

As I said, I developed eczema all over my legs, which I later found out was caused by stress. My stepfather was sexually abusing me and it affected me so much on the inside that it showed on my skin. I wore baggy clothes so he couldn't see my figure. I tried everything to get him to stop. I hated him. And I had to keep it all inside, and keep it all together. This was eating me up and the eczema showed what I was going through on the inside. These were some of the most challenging times of my life. I couldn't stand to be around him. Family members couldn't figure out why my stepfather and I weren't close. They automatically blamed me and called me a spoiled brat. I allowed them to assume whatever they wanted. If he wouldn't leave, then as soon as I was able to, I would disappear.

I started to withdraw. I isolated myself. I would write stories in my diary to escape reality. I felt so alone. I looked at my sister and she was happy. She had her father. They all acted normal like nothing was happening. My mom was pretending. Everybody liked him — family, friends, everyone. They were all fooled. I couldn't stand being in the same room with him. My sister looked just like him. I needed to get out of that house. I just didn't know how.

How did my mom feel about her husband being attracted to her daughter? Did she start to dislike me? Did she feel any jealousy or negativity towards me? Did she hate me?

JAI HUDSON

More and more I felt like I had to get out of there. I was causing the disruption, not country. I couldn't pretend. I started to think sexual abuse was normal. With my mother knowing every time it happened, and doing nothing to stop it, I started to feel like maybe something was wrong with me. I couldn't just go with the flow. So because I couldn't accept the abuse and act like nothing was happening, there was friction in the house. But I always felt deep in my heart I didn't deserve what was happening to me.

So much anger grew in me. I remember one evening before my mom and her husband got home from work, I went into their bedroom. I didn't know what I was looking for but something led me to my mother's bed. I walked over to the right side, which was my stepfather's side of the bed. I kneeled down and peeked under the bed at a small, gray, metal box. I pulled it slowly towards me. I opened the box and saw exactly what I was looking for. Something I saw in action movies, even heard the sound it made at the Brevoort basketball games when one of the teams lost. I even had a plastic one for my Nintendo duck hunt game. But this one was different. It was real and right in front of me.

I thought to myself, I was going to shoot him and save my mother and sister — just like it happened in the movies. I was going to stop this once and for all. I picked it up and held the gun in my hands. I remember thinking to myself that it was not very appealing. It was dull black and gray, with several scratches and it looked real beat up. I mean, really, did I expect it to look pretty while doing something so serious as hurting someone? I picked it up and held it firmly within my two adolescent hands to get comfortable with it.

JAI HUDSON

If I was going to do what I planned, I had to be calm. Did it have bullets already? Would he die? Then I thought to myself, *I should do it when he falls asleep.* I will take it in my room now and wake up in the middle of the night and shoot him. I then realized I didn't think my plan completely through. Should I just shoot myself? It seemed like I was the problem anyway. I could just take me out of the equation. My mom and sister could be happy and not worry about me disclosing the secret. With me gone everything could be better.

Of course, at that moment, something came over me. It was like an air came over me totally changing my mind. I put the gun down. I couldn't do this. I didn't know why I thought differently but I did and I didn't even battle this new feeling. It didn't feel like the thing I should do. So I put the gun back in the box, closed it, and slid it back under the

bed. I got up and walked back into my room.
I had to think of another plan.

RESENTMENT

Maybe that's when I started to resent my
mom. How could she put such a grown-up
situation and decision on me — her child? I
grew to be very angry and I continuously felt
like I wasn't good enough, or worthy. I wasn't
important enough to save me from what I
was experiencing. Then I started to think I
must be the worst person on earth because
my own mother didn't care enough to stop it.
My mom didn't put me first. And I didn't put
me first either. I thought about killing him. I
thought about killing myself. Maybe I could
poison him. Maybe I should take a whole
bottle of Tylenol. I felt I should just
disappear. I hated him, I hated her, and I
hated me.

JAI HUDSON

My mother told me to be quiet about it. So I did just that! I endured the abuse, kept quiet, and tried to think of a master plan of how I could get this man to stop sexually abusing me and still have my mother close. How I could escape this world I was in that created a thick cloud of sadness inside? I started to learn that I couldn't have it all. Everything has its price.

One night a stray bullet came through the window in the living room where I was doing my homework and landed three feet away from the chair I was sitting in. That night I wished it had hit me. I was just so unhappy. I told myself my voice and feelings didn't matter anymore anyway. I wasn't heard, so I started to be quiet. I went from being called "mouthy" and "talkative" to being called quiet and an introvert. How ironic!

JAI HUDSON

V

FACTS

"If you are truly seeking wisdom and growth, you must spread knowledge, you must teach." – Yehuda Berg

SEXUAL ABUSE: *What is It?*

According to Wikipedia, the child sexual abuse and the Psychological affects section: **"Child sexual abuse or child molestation** is a form of child abuse in which an adult or older adolescent uses a child for sexual stimulation. Forms of child sexual abuse include asking or pressuring a child to engage in sexual activities (regardless of the outcome), indecent exposure (of the genitals, female nipples, etc.) to a child with intent to gratify their own sexual desires or to intimidate or groom the child, physical sexual contact with a child, or using a child to produce child pornography."

Sexual Abuse has been around forever. It may have been called something else in the past but it's all the same. Abuse in general can be physical, emotional, or mental. This topic creates a silence amongst society and families around the world. It's one of those things we haven't been able to get under control. Not only is it not effectively handled, but no one likes to talk about it. We not only silence the victim, but we do not socially address the harms and effects.

SEXUAL ABUSE NOW

Sexual Abuse is traumatic. Sexual Abuse toward a child is even more detrimental. Now with the advancement of technology, it has become too easy for a predator to find its victim. Because this is an everyday dilemma, we need to address it and deal with the consequences head on. If we can't prevent it from happening we need to help the victims rise above their circumstances. We have 1.9+ million abused kids in the U.S. growing up to be dysfunctional human beings, trying so desperately to navigate through life without the proper tools. Then they are having kids who in turn are abused, and they can't even save them because they don't have the necessary skills needed to do so.

Here are some additional statistics from the National Department of Justice U.S. Raising Awareness about Sexual Abuse Facts and Statistics:

· Approximately 30% of sexual assault cases are reported to authorities.

· 9.3% of cases of maltreatment of children in 2012 were classified as sexual abuse.

· 62,939 cases of child sexual abuse were reported in 2012.

· According to the Bureau of Justice Statistics' National Criminal Victimization Survey, in 2012, there were 346,830 reported rapes or sexual assaults of persons 12 years or older.

· In 2010, 12% of rapes and sexual assaults involved a weapon.

In 2010, 25% of the female victims of rape/sexual assault were victimized by strangers.

In a 2012 maltreatment report, of the victims who were sexually abused:

26% were in the age group of 12–14 years and 34% were younger than 9 years.

Approximately 1.8 million adolescents in the United States have been the victims of sexual assault. Research conducted by the Centers for Disease Control (CDC) estimates that approximately:

- 1 in 6 boys and 1 in 4 girls are sexually abused before the age of 18.

- 35.8% of sexual assaults occur when the victim is between the ages of 12 and 17.

-82% of all juvenile victims are female.

-69% of the teen sexual assaults reported to law enforcement occurred in the residence of the victim, the offender, or another individual.
-Teens 16 to 19 years of age were 3 ½ times more likely than the general population to be victims of rape, attempted rape, or sexual assault.
-Approximately 1 in 5 female high school students report being physically and/or sexually abused by a dating partner.

Males suffer from sexual abuse too. According to the Center for Disease Control, they estimate that one in six boys are sexually abused before the age of 18. In 82% of sexual abuse cases the victims are females. Approximately 1.8 million adolescents in the United States have been the victims of sexual assault.

"Take, for instance, a K–12 school district with 500 female and 500 male students. More than 100 female and 50 male students in this system have experienced sexual abuse. Assuming the victims are distributed evenly across grades, then there are approximately eight female and four male victims of sexual abuse at each grade level. So, if we teach seventh-grade literature, we may have as many as 12 victims of sexual abuse throughout our classes." Tracy K. Cruise wrote this, in "The Sexual Abuse of Children and Adolescent."

It is heartbreaking to know that this is still happening. Children are still waking up from bad dreams and kids are still being manipulated. Children are still suffering.

MOLESTATION – *What Is It?*

"Child molestation is an everyday situation in this country as well as all across the world. Where once it was an isolated issue, it has now become an every day occurrence.

JAI HUDSON

If proper healing does not take place, molestation destroys the person — both male and female. It can even destroy a family. But when exactly have we seen proper healing take place? Proper healing, requires intimate knowledge of the effects of abuse on the soul and the psyche. In molestation, the victims are many, not only the child in question, but the mother also. Molestation has nothing to do with sex. It has everything to do with someone exerting their power and control over another. Molestation is the raping of one's very soul. Acceptance of the effects is just the seed of what needs to be understood if healing is to take place.

The effects of molestation do not end upon completion of the act. They follow the victim throughout life. The effects are many and are played out in many different ways in the person's life. The effect of molestation, rape or abuse touches on the insecurities of every family member." – "Recovery from sexual abuse, rape and molestation," from the Self Empowerment and Development Center.

EFFECTS OF ABUSE

When a child is raped, sexually abused or molested, the effects are many: shame, feeling unlovable, not good enough, dirty, feels everyone knows, inability to trust, distrust authority, unsatisfying sex, distrust of men / women, hide behind barriers, low self-esteem, non engagement in life, the male or female psyche is severely damaged, obesity, anorexia, inappropriate sexual beliefs and behavior, only good enough to be used for sexual gratification, can't be themselves, have to be another to be accepted, have to do things to be accepted by others, deny themselves, are often not present, have to carry family secrets, have great difficulty in saying no or putting healthy boundaries in place with people, etc., etc. The list is endless. Every victim is different. This is just a sampling of the belief systems that we victims have taken on about ourselves. This needs to be addressed and the abused healed.

"Sexual abuse can affect a child both short and long term. Some experience depression, anxiety, eating disorders, poor self-esteem, sleep disturbances, advanced sexual activity, inappropriate sexual knowledge and post-traumatic stress disorders. Approximately 30% of sexual assault cases are reported to authorities. 62,939 cases of child sexual abuse were reported in 2012." (US Department of Justice: "Raising Awareness about Sexual Abuse Facts and Statistics.")

The American Psychiatric Association states "children cannot consent to sexual activity with adults," and condemns any such action by an adult: "An adult who engages in sexual activity with a child is performing a criminal and immoral act which never can be considered normal or socially acceptable behavior."

Rape and sexual abuse has long-term emotional consequences that can lead to depression and in some cases suicide. It is quite common for victims to suffer from depression. Untreated depression is the number one cause for suicide. About 33% of abused victims have suicidal thoughts. About 13% of victims will attempt suicide. Suicide attempts can occur years after the rape.

Overall, participants with no history of childhood abuse were less likely to demonstrate suicidal behavior than those who had been abused. Analysis shows that the non-abused group had a lower prevalence of lifetime suicide attempts (6.0%) than the physical abuse (11.7%), sexual abuse (14.8%), and both abuse (32.2%) groups.

The study also indicates that the risk of suicide later in life is related to the frequency of abuse during childhood and the identity of the abuser.

WHO ARE THE ABUSERS?

Only about 10% of perpetrators of child sexual abuse are strangers to the child. They are family members, family friends, babysitters, neighbors etc. First, abuse by a father or is considered especially traumatic, because such abuse is more likely to occur in families with multiple problems. These families cannot provide safe and healing conditions following abuse. So there are several dysfunctions stacked on top of one another. It becomes normal for family members to ignore this mountain of problems, as if it's not even there. This speaks volumes to the kids and the abused.

WHAT WOULD YOU DO?

What if the abuser is your husband or boyfriend? It's easy to say you would go to the cops or you would confront him. If you confront him and he denies it, then what? This has been an issue in many households from the beginning of time. Then if the abuser is in power and offers money to quiet the situation, more and more damage is created. It seems like it can make you feel like you will fail without him so its usually swept under the rug and never really addressed at all.

There's a tradition of "keep family business within the family" when sexual abuse is involved. Often times the abused won't tell anyone, fearing they won't be believed and protected. According to the US Department of Justice, Facts and Statistics, disclosure of sexual abuse is often delayed. Children often avoid telling because they are either afraid of a negative reaction from their parents or being harmed by the abuser. Therefore, disclosure is delayed until adulthood.

Is it fear, is it tradition, is it lack of knowledge, is it the dirty little secrets swept under the rug and repeated generation after generation? Victims are manipulated by their abusers. They are made to feel that it's their fault. That one feeling starts a domino effect of more negative feelings.

Regardless of the circumstances, a child loves and needs to be with his or her parents, especially their mother. There is an instinctive bond that cannot be broken.

JAI HUDSON

Although a child should be removed from the home for their own protection, this adds more grief, on top of the other unmanageable burdens that the child must bear. Simultaneously, the child starts to believe it is their fault. Then sometimes authorities take it even further by placing responsibility on the victim, insinuating or accusing that it is somehow their behavior or appearance that triggered the abuse. This confuses and magnifies feelings inside. Because a child usually feels discord in the home is their fault, by blaming the victim those feelings have been reinforced. – US Department of Justice, Facts and Statistics.

HOW DO THE MOTHERS FEEL?

Some mothers stay with their men even after finding out the same man raped or sexually abused their child. I've realized as a woman, you have to be strong to stay, and you need even more strength to leave. We all need support. It's a catch-22. Staying in a relationship with a man who suffers from a disease of harming children creates a dead end either way you look at it. Everyone involved needs healing. But of course, that is not usually the medicine of choice. Staying verses overcoming manipulation and fear and saving your child from sexual abuse becomes a lifelong dilemma. Most times, the mothers have been abused themselves.

Though I don't wish psychological problems on anyone, the wives of pedophiles should be accountable for having suspicions but dismissing them to protect their husbands or the status quo. Anxiety is a lot easier to deal with than prison time. My hope for the future is that the wives of pedophiles who haven't yet been caught get honest about their suspicions and actually do something about it.

JAI HUDSON

The majority of the time, the victims of sexual abuse are left to clean up the mess. Some are lucky and receive therapy. Some are forgotten and expected to fix their problems themselves. There needs to be more emphasis on the psychological effects on the victim. Not only does the abuse affect the victim emotionally and mentally, but if we do not address the effects, we are adding to the vicious cycle. Abused children grow to be abused adults, in turn having children who experience abuse. And guess what? The parents didn't receive the proper healing so how do we expect change? How do we break the cycle of abuse? The only way is to heal.

Society tends to focus on the abuser and developing antidotes to prevent other abuse. Millions of dollars are spent on developing homes and databases for sexual offenders. So many programs are being developed to reform sex offenders. Which is totally helpful and needed to attempt to decrease future cases of abuse. However, what about the abuse that has already occurred? What about those victims? We have to remember the disease of a sexual abuser didn't start with the specific act of abuse. The sex offender most likely was abused or witnessed some form of abuse. It's a cycle, and until we add some focus on healing the victims, we will continually have victims who become enablers of sex offenses. We have kids growing up to be adults, with so much damage done to their soul and mind. With the extensive list of after-effects from sexual abuse and increasing suicide rates, we need to meet this problem head on.

STATISTICS

The effects of child sexual abuse can include depression,[6] post-traumatic stress disorder,[7] anxiety,[8] complex post-traumatic stress disorder,[9] propensity to further victimization in adulthood,[10] and physical injury to the child, among other problems.[11] Sexual abuse by a family member is a form of incest and can result in more serious and long-term psychological trauma, especially in the case of parental incest.[12]

The global prevalence of child sexual abuse has been estimated at 19.7% for females and 7.9% for males, according to a 2009 study published in Clinical Psychology Review that examined 65 studies from 22 countries. Using the available data, the highest prevalence rate of child sexual abuse geographically was found in Africa (34.4%), primarily because of high rates in South Africa; Europe showed the lowest prevalence rate (9.2%); America and Asia had prevalence rates between 10.1% and 23.9%.[13] In the past, other research has concluded similarly that in North America, for example, approximately 15% to 25% of women and 5% to 15% of men were sexually abused when they were children.

Most sexual abuse offenders are acquainted with their victims; approximately 30% are relatives of the child, most often brothers, fathers, uncles or cousins; around 60% are other acquaintances, such as "friends" of the family, babysitters, or neighbors; strangers are the offenders in approximately 10% of child sexual abuse cases.[14] Most child sexual abuse is committed by men; studies show that women commit 14% to 40% of offenses reported against boys and 6% of offenses reported against girls.

JAI HUDSON

VI
FEARLESS

JAI HUDSON

"CLOSER"

Song by Goapele

Closer to my dreams
It's coming over me
I'm gettin' higher
Closer to my dreams
I'm getting higher and higher
Feel it in my sleep
Some times it feels like I'll never go pass here
Some times it feels like I'm stuck forever and ever
But, I'm going higher
Closer to my dreams
I'm goin' higher and higher
I can almost reach
Some times you just have to let it go (Let it go, let it
go)
Leaving all my fears to burn down
Push them all away so I can move on
Closer to my dreams
Feel it all over my being
Close your eyes and see what you believe
I'm happy as long as we 're apart
Then I'm moving on to my dreams
I'll be moving higher (Moving higher)
Closer to my dreams
And higher and higher, higher
Feel it in my being (I can feel it flow around me)
I know that I could not go alone (No, no)
I'm moving higher (Higher), oh...
I'm going higher and higher and higher (Higher and

JAI HUDSON

I'M A FRESH-MAN

In 1993 I started high school. I attended the HS of Telecommunications Arts and Technology in Bayridge, BK. HSTAT was a very small school with about 1000 students in total. During the first few days of school I stayed to myself. I was in a whole new world. I knew only two or three kids from middle school. I wanted to go to a school where I knew no one and I could be me. So HSTAT was perfect.

One day in gym class I was playing basketball with my teacher Mr. T. I will admit, I was showing off a little. In basketball, I was known for my dribble, drive, and 3-point shot. I played the point guard position. Learning how to shake my opponent using my dribble was my specialty. So Mr. T and I played a little one-on-one. He guarded me and I guarded him. He stopped before throwing the ball and said to me, "You are really good." He didn't know that before high school I played basketball on BedStuy's basketball courts, studying some of the best young local basketball stars in my neighborhood — Michael Payton, Trevor Diggs, etc. Michael Jordan was the greatest player in the NBA in my eyes. Basketball was my outlet. I went to the basketball courts to watch the games for hours. By studying my neighborhood greats I learned flashy moves, the best defense strategies, and the perfect form for connecting successful shots. I was a sponge.

The summer before high school I made the decision I wasn't going play on the HS team. Back then, the basketball games in Brooklyn seemed to always end with a fight. The opposing teams were either sore losers or *egomaniacs*. I was so tired of fighting; I wanted to enjoy life. I was also ready to embrace my femininity.

JAI HUDSON

A few days after my one-on-one with Mr. T, the high school's basketball coach, Ms. D, pulled me out of class and took me to the student office. She wanted to meet me and see if I was interested in playing on the varsity basketball team. *Here we go again,* I said to myself. There were other players in the student office that day. That's the first time I met Talia Parkinson. She was the only one who said something to me at the time. She said, "You should join the team." How did they know I could play? Then I realized it was from my gym teacher who I played basketball with a few days before in class.

Because it was a varsity team and I was a freshman, I had to be granted eligibility. There were three weeks of doctor visits and getting papers signed to become eligible to play. I was extremely nervous, but I sucked it up because the whole team was counting on me, it seemed. That put a lot of fear in me,

JAI HUDSON

because not only did I not like that type of attention but it was like *all eyes on me* — time to show and prove.

In the locker room I listened to certain songs to prepare me for the court. I listened *to* Onyx – "Throw your guns in the air and Slam," Run DMC – "Down with the King," Wu-Tang Clan – "Chessboxin'," Black Moon –"Don't front I got you open," Lords of the Underground – "Chief Rocka," Biggie and Jay Z –"Brooklyn's Finest" and Biggie and Method Man – "The What." These songs made me feel powerful and if I had to show and prove, they prepared me for war.

When I finally stepped on the court it was pandemonium. My first game I scored 10 points and 5 assists. My team had a horrible record with no wins. There was a lot of pressure on me. My jersey number was 14. I played the point guard position and sometimes the right guard. Coach D gave us a number of plays to run. One play in particular that caused discomfort was the "Red play." This play was when all the players spread out along the sides of the court and my opponent and I are face to face with a clear path to the basket. *All eyes on me.* That type of attention made me feel super uncomfortable. But discomfort usually brings lessons and growth, right? And at the end of it all, challenges usually fueled me. Even with the nervous feelings, it pushed me to overcome.

HSTAT VS. BROOKLYN TECH AWAY, 4ᵀᴴ QUARTER

Brooklyn Tech's point guard was a short Asian girl who was considered one of the strongest point guards in my division. Everybody loved her. We were defending ourselves against one of the strongest teams. The whistle blew, and the ball was passed to me. I dribbled a short distance looking down the court to strategize my offence. Then suddenly Coach D yelled out "RED!" Of course she would call that play. But anyway, I focused on Brooklyn Tech's star point guard. Just me and her down the court. It felt like everyone disappeared. We were eye-to-eye. She mirrored my every move. The pressure was on. *I had to do something fast and score*, I thought to myself. She played me super close and did not let up.

This immediately took me back to Brevoort basketball court. Being a female and a tomboy made the guys feel like they needed to guard me extra hard. They didn't want to be embarrassed by a girl. But the flip side was that I developed a strong dribble. Up until now I never really displayed my dribbling ability. I didn't want to be called a show-off; I loved to win but I never liked embarrassing someone in the process.

Brooklyn Tech's star player guarded me, showing me why she was considered one of the strongest point guards in Brooklyn. I turned around with my back to her and pushed her back with my body, however she was still guarding me close. Her defense was top notch. Yeah, I was a little scared. But fear always fueled me. Besides, I had been guarded by tougher.

The crowd was cheering for her because she was their hero and booing at me every time I tried to shake her. My team was also in "their house" so they had the home court advantage. This was nerve-racking. We continued this down the court until I could finally I can see the basket over my shoulder. That's when I turned back around to face her. That's when I envisioned Allen Iverson *crossing the ball over* crushing his opponent. Then suddenly I heard a voice say, "Do it." So I crossed the ball over low, threw the ball between my legs, faked to the left, then crossed behind my back, and then finally I lost her and she fell. Yes she fell to the floor, allowing me to head to the basket. She didn't know which way I was going and lost her balance. I lost her, or as they say in the hood "*I broke her ankles.*" I then charged for the basket and laid it up. *I Scored*!! Wow, I did it. I scored on Brooklyn Tech's star player.

The fear inside was so real. But I faced it and was victorious. We didn't win the game, but my peers praised me and the newspapers did too. I faced a huge fear of having all eyes and pressure on me. From that point on I was unstoppable —scoring 20, 30, 40, 50 points, triple doubles and all. We didn't win the division title or anything but at least we had wins under our belt.

JAI HUDSON

At this time in my life, I would say I was an Oscar winning actress because I had to act like nothing was wrong. I had to act as if I liked my stepfather, didn't resent my mother, and we were one big happy family. I became uncomfortable around men. I could see the same look that was in country's eyes, in the eyes of other men. I had an attraction for boys my age, but it got weird when the males were older and if things became overly sexual. I also started to wear baggy clothes, played basketball, and became more and more tomboyish.

I didn't want to see my beauty. I felt like when I expressed my femininity it created the wrong attention in my household. So this became a habit. Not seeing my beauty and not being comfortable expressing it either. I was left to protect myself by any means necessary as a child. It just so happens that the means I chose was to close up and not recognize my beauty.

I thought if I didn't care about myself, and hid from the world, I could be invisible. I carried these feelings throughout life. I started to feel like attention created monsters. That's what I experienced and that scared me. I never looked in the mirror. I never really had any pride in myself. My family downplayed physical appearance anyway. I knew I was attractive, but I felt like I had to cover that up. I feared attention. I feared being free again.

"HAT 2 DA BACK"

Song by TLC

Being that I am the kinda girl that I am
Nobody can make me do what I don't want to
I can be myself a lot and I'm proud of what I got
So I'll never change for you
Being that I am the kinda girl that I am
Tight jeans don't hit the scene with one like me
I got to feeling free and you better believe I'll
Do what pleases me
Yo Left Eye kick the scene
See everyday last week and not a place to go
This nut still had me dressin' like a fashion show
But not this week I'm chillin' cause it's nothin' to hide
Threw on my baggy dips and waited for my ride
He pulled up knock knock till I opened the door
Peeped my gear and started dissin' me from head to
toe
But yo just to let you know, it's takin'
Make me wanna say gotta go, gotta go
Hat 2 da back
I gotta keep my pants down real low
That's the kinda girl I am
That's the kinda girl I am
Hat 2 da back
I gotta kick my pants down real low
That's the kinda girl that I am
Here we go, here we go, here we go again
Being that I am the kinda girl that I am

Some people just don't understand the things I do
Chillin' with the girls or kick it with the fellas
If I choose
Being that I am the kinda girl that I am
Dumb rules are left for fools
With no attitude I think my way is cool
So let me be me and continue being smooth

JAI HUDSON

VII
FAITH

"FAITH INTERLUDE"

Song by Faith Evans

I have the faith

That can move any mountain

Faith

That can conquer

Anything

JAI HUDSON

A WAY OUT

Toward the end of my freshman year of high school, my Uncle St Clair passed away. St Clair was my favorite uncle. He was super smart. We connected in a way that was special because I felt like he truly listened to how I felt. He championed me and made me feel like my feelings did matter. He didn't know about my abuse, but I sensed he knew something wasn't right. My uncle spent his last days very close to my mom and me. It was like he was there to help with the nighttime. He'd come over every night after I got out of school. We'd sit in the living room and talk about everything from robots to my fascination with Japan, to reciting songs I wrote to solving the toughest math problem.

After my uncle's passing my mom decided to purchase a house. Because my uncle and I were so close, I got the feeling he wrote me into his will. My mom asked me,

"Where did I want to move?" I was so happy she asked me and would consider my choice. However, I didn't have to think long, I immediately replied, "Rosedale Queens." That's where Talia lived. So my mom and I went house hunting in Rosedale for homes. We moved into this big blue house on 221 Street, a tree-lined block with predominantly middle- class West Indian families. My room was located in the attic so it was away from everyone. I loved my new room. I decorated my room with huge posters of TLC, Aaliyah, Mary J Blige, Jodeci, KrisKross, Janet Jackson, the hottest cars, and the greatest entertainer ever — Michael Jackson.

Dedicated to my Uncle, St Clair:
"GEORGIE PORGIE"

Song by M.C. Lyte

Wished I Woulda Told Him How I Liked Him So Much
How He Made Me Feel With The Slightest Touch
Now He's Gone And I Can't Tell Him Nothin
Wish He Was Here So I Could Say Somethin
The Story Is Not To Say That I'm In Sorrow
Just To Say No One Is Promise Tomorrow
If You Love Someone You Should Say It Often
You Never Know When They'll Be Layin In A Coffin
Wake Up, It's Important That You Know That
No One On Earth Is Promised Tomorrow
Believe That!
And Don't Think That It Can't Happen To You
'Kissed The Girls And Made Them Cry"
Can It Be I've Stayed Away Too Long'
Can It Be I've Stayed Away Too Long
"Kissed The Girls And Made Them Cry'

When we moved to Rosedale, the abuse magically stopped. My room was now located in the attic of the house. So it was very difficult for him to get to me. That was such a blessing. Thank you Uncle St Clair.

I developed an attitude like I could do whatever I wanted now because I had dealt with the pain for so many years. I became a little rebellious. I'd invite boys over, friends over, stay out for days, ignore country completely, and eventually I moved into Talia's house. I didn't feel like I needed permission to do anything. No one cared before so now that I was older and out of that house of control I could do what I wanted. I had a certain aura during this time. I just got my license, had an incredibly handsome boyfriend named Geoffrey Garcy, an amazing best friend, a family at Talia's house, and I was starting to be happy.

JAI HUDSON

One day I went over to my mother's house in Queens to grab some clothes. When I arrived I realized she was at work, but country was there. I walked in the house and saw him sitting in the living room. He called out my name and asked me to come into the living room. I came to the doorway but I didn't respond at all. He said, "Jacquetta, why do you hate me?" I looked at him like he had two heads. But I didn't respond. Then he said, "I mean, how could you blame me?" I interrupted him immediately by responding, "What? Are you serious?" I then turned around to leave. I did not want to have this conversation at all.... not now anyway. I exited the room and left the house. I couldn't believe he just asked me a question like that. And then asked how could I blame him? I couldn't understand what was happening at all. All I know is that it made my skin crawl to be around him. I did

not want to sit and have a conversation with
him about anything. I wasn't ready. All of my
family were fooled by country. He was extra
nice and friendly to everyone. I was dealing
with all of these secrets and unhealthy
emotions. My family started to view me as
the problem. Because they didn't know the
big secret, country seemed like the good guy
and I was the unruly brat. I allowed them to
feel this way, because I had bigger issues on
my plate. My plan was to just stay away.

GOD STEPPED IN

Talia and I became very close friends. Talia
lived in Rosedale Queens with her mother
and little sister. I spent a lot of time at her
house. Being in their home felt very familiar.
It was all females in the house. It made me
think of how it could have been if my mother
had made my stepfather leave. Talia and I
were attached at the hip. I was very quiet

and shy and Talia became a motivation to push forward. Once I moved to Rosedale, I basically stayed at Talia's house. It was a way I could get away from my family — *the perfect escape.*

School was super important to us. Because I had gotten good grades in middle school, I was offered the opportunity to graduate high school a year early. Crazy thing is Talia skipped 6th grade also, so she was a sophomore when I got to high school. So what that all meant was I could graduate with my best friend. That meant I would graduate high school in three years. Of course I wanted to graduate early! When I made that decision, I was featured in the Daily News for Student Athlete of the month. We did everything together. We travelled to New York City every day for school via the Long Island Railroad. Every Friday we took the N train to the West Village to shop and discover new restaurants. We went to the Atrium to buy the newest DKNY clothing. We would also have dinner at our favorite Chinese restaurant on Bleecker Street. We were 16 years old doing such grown up things. We were mature 16 year olds, but very respectful.

Sonia was from the island of Jamaica. Her accent was so strong. Sonia is a Gemini like me. During the time I stayed with Sonia, Talia, and her little sister Alisha, I was exposed to the Jamaican culture. I learned a lot about being a woman from Sonia and Talia. My family was from Barbados, so I had been around Caribbean culture but Jamaicans were a little different. Sonia took Talia and Alisha to Jamaica every year, and this year they invited me. We went to Ocho Rios first. I climbed Duns River Falls, stayed at the JFK resort, went snorkeling, learned to swim a little, and learned so much about the culture. Then we went to Kingston, Jamaica. Kingston was totally different from Ocho Rios. I loved the rawness and "hood" feeling Kingston gave me. These were the "native" people of Jamaica — the heart of the island. I experienced kids showing us the new Jamaican dances, buying box lunch from the lady down the street, saw Buju Banton perform, and even went to the jungle. The jungle is a place in Kingston where it is tremendously poverty-stricken. It was so dark and gloomy. Dogs were treated as garbage disposals instead of pets. However, there was so much love and culture there. They welcomed me in a way that made me feel like I was Jamaican too. We stayed in Jamaica for two weeks and it was an amazing trip that I will never forget.

I was so happy to be away from my dysfunctional house and be around a family who loved me and made me feel special. I

JAI HUDSON

remember when I first decided to confide in Talia with the biggest secret I kept. She was my best friend, the person who understood me and championed me. I had to finally get this out. I was so nervous but I knew somehow I would feel better. I thought about it for a while before I actually said anything.

I remember we were in Talia's bedroom, and if I remember correctly, she was in the mirror doing her hair. I said, "Talia I have to tell you something." I felt she opened her home to me, she included me in her world, and I couldn't keep lying about why I hated my stepfather. I couldn't keep lying about why my mom and I weren't close. I couldn't keep lying about a family that I never felt close to.

So I closed my eyes and said the words I had been running away from and keeping inside. I told her the secret. "I was molested." She was shocked. Silence hung in the air and then she asked, "Who hurt you?" I responded, "My stepfather." She immediately hugged me and let me know that I had a place in her family. I felt like a huge lump disappeared from my throat. I felt like a weight was lifted. I felt so much better telling my best friend about my abuse.

In 1996 I graduated high school and attended Syracuse University with my best friend Talia Parkinson. When I received my acceptance letter I was so happy SU accepted me. Syracuse was my first choice as far as colleges I had applied to. The first person I called was Talia, and funny thing is she was calling me at the same time to tell me she had been accepted as well. I was so happy to be accepted by a great school like Syracuse University. I couldn't believe this was really happening. I was actually going to college. It was a great moment for me.

JAI HUDSON

Immediately, a fear jumped inside of me. It wasn't fear of change, because as you can see change was normal to me. For some strange reason, I feared telling my mom. I don't know why I was afraid, but when I told her I was accepted by Syracuse, her reaction confirmed my feelings. Her response to me was: "You can't go to Syracuse, I can't afford it." Her response hurt my feelings. I worked so hard to get where I was, enduring all that I went through, and that was her response? Not a *congratulations baby* or even a warm embrace. I was crushed. I started to think, *Why is this happening to me*? I felt like I had suffered enough as far as what happened with country, so why was she creating these roadblocks?

Of course, her negative response fueled me. Because I hadn't received my award letter yet, I had no idea how much I needed to pay to attend SU. She was assuming she couldn't afford it instead of celebrating an important time with me. When I received my award package of scholarships and grants, I was given enough money to cover the entire tuition. The balance after the aid I was granted was only $1000 a semester. So my mother responded as harsh as she did without this knowledge. And I didn't tell her what my award package was either. She wasn't happy for me so I kept everything pertaining to college to myself. I immediately got to work. I called my Aunt Shanecka (my father's sister) and told her what happened. She responded with what I needed at the moment. Not only would she help me, she was so happy for me. She even sent a limo to pick me up with my friends and celebrate my birthday and acceptance to college. We went to City Island in the Bronx.

JAI HUDSON

August of 1996 I was preparing to go to Syracuse University to embark on a life-changing experience. However, I did feel guilty about leaving my mother and sister behind in Queens NY with the monster. But I didn't know what else to do. Was I not supposed to go and live my life? I was happy to get away from home, but I didn't want my mom to continue to suffer and my sister to witness so much dysfunction. Something as wonderful as going away to college became such a heavy burden in my heart.

My mother threw me a big going away party. I think she felt bad about her reaction when I was accepted. She printed a big poster with my graduation picture on it. Everyone who attended the celebration wrote a message to me. The messages were so touching. I was so happy. Everyone was there, my newly appointed godmother Valerie, Ann, my godbrothers Naquan and

Larry, Johnesha, Debra and Johnny, Ronnie, Niesha, and KJ, all my friends and family. Talia even came. It was beautiful. I felt so special.

"YOU GOT ME"
Song By The Roots & Erykah Badu

If you were worried 'bout where
I been or who I saw or
What club I went to with my homies
Baby don't worry you know that you got me
If you were worried 'bout where
I been or who I saw or
What club I went to with my homies
Baby don't worry you know that you got me

JAI HUDSON

Talia gave me the name Jai. We were like *twin souls*. Talia could see my heart, She saw me. She was the type of friend I needed at that time. We gave each other names. Her name was Tai and mine was Jai. I don't know where Talia got that name from, but ever since she named me Jai, my life changed forever. Jai means Victorious —the perfect name for me. I didn't know it back then, but Jai was the name I more identified with. It allowed me to dream big (victorious) and always aim for my name's meaning. It felt like I was a new person and I could experience a new beginning.

Talia was super feminine and I had a tomboyish style. We dressed alike sometimes, however we individually gave off a different style. I always had a unique sense of style, however, I wasn't as confident in my style because all the other girls were more feminine. There was something about expressing myself through my style that created a sense of liberation. I felt like I was truly me being me.

The year was 1996, oversized plaid Tommy Hilfiger shirts, Durango boots, Silver DKNY bubble, combat boots, oversized hockey jerseys, Matrix-looking sunglasses, Olympic Jordan's, Bamboo earrings smashed in, Baggy boyfriend jeans with tommy Hilfiger boxers peeking thru, and oversized jean suits; the style during the late 90s had changed a little. Back then it was accepted for women to wear oversized clothing: "the boyfriend look." Musical artists like TLC, Janet Jackson, Mary J Blige, Aaliyah and Total were making "tomboy" sexy. Fashion in the 1990s was right up my alley. I loved to be creative. I loved to express my style. Style and music went together in my opinion. I was inspired by music as I was inspired by style and culture. When I hear music I am automatically bought back to a place in my mind and I can always envision the fashion. Something so small as a song or style of clothing can bring you back to a happy place in the past. I also can feel what I felt at that time. That's so magical.

"WHAT ABOUT US?"

Song by Total

What about you, what about me
What about us, what we gon' do
Total help me sing, total help me sing
What about you, what about me
What about us, what we gon' do

NEVER GIVE UP

Music in the late 90s was explosive. The West coast had Dr. Dre and Snoop, Tupac and Deathrow, Rage ad Yoyo. I loved the music coming from the west. It was such a breath of fresh air. The South was also inspiring. Jermaine Dupree, Usher, TLC, Teddy Riley, Pharrell, Timberland and Missy, as well as others contributed to the sound of the "dirty south." During this time NYC was also contributing heavily to the sound of music as a whole. The Wutang and Rocafella Records movement was setting the tone for the NYC vibe musically. Then there was Badboy Entertainment dominating the lifestyle, music, and culture fusion in NYC. Mary J Blige, Jodeci, Total, Faith Evans, 112, Craig Mack, Junior mafia with Lil Kim, Mace, and the most incredible rapper Notorious BIG were bridging the gap between lifestyle and music. It was a specific *energy in New York that may sound a little cliché but the movement made me proud to be from NYC. New York City was on fire.*

Back then we used to record TV shows onto VHS tapes. That's what we did to keep memories of award show and special videos aired on TV. I remember sitting close to the TV holding the record and play button simultaneously to record the *Source awards and Urban Aid award show. Puff Daddy presents the Bad Boy Family. Biggie in the King Chair, Total doing their dance to "Cant you see," hearing the magnetic voice of Faith Evans flowing to her song "You used to love me." Badboy movement then closed the show with the introduction of Junior Mafia featuring Lil' Kim. Mary J Blige straight from Uptown Records sang "Everyday it rains," in her head-to-toe Fendi outfit. The crowd took out their umbrellas and sang along to the words.*

JAI HUDSON

This was such a great time in music for New York City. It was culturally impactful and socially inspiring. These artists were from NYC, which meant they were from where I was from, which also meant my dream was even more attainable. Seeing Jay Z, Notorious BIG, Lil Kim (her mom worked with my mom at HPD) on televised award shows was so inspirational. They were from BedStuy also. They were taking the culture to new heights and more mainstream. Dressed in all black and leather, the style was so regal yet *"ghetto fabulous"* at the same time. The term "ghetto fabulous" was established. If you were in NYC during these days, there was no way you didn't feel the powerful energy that music created.

When I went to college I basically stayed away from my home. When I came home from school I stayed at Talia's house and most times my mother didn't even know I was in Queens. In college I was in heaven. I felt grown up and I was having a lot of fun. It was such an amazing experience. Students on campus called Talia and me the "DKNY Twins." All that DKNY we had purchased over the years had become a nickname for us. When we stepped on campus, I would say we caused a small uproar. Not to toot our own horns, but we were two pretty, smart, and stylish girls from NYC in a place like Syracuse NY. It was just a great feeling being at college and being welcomed for who we were.

Initially I went to college to study radio, television, and film. I wanted to create films and music. However, I took a class in fashion design as an elective and it sparked my interest. So, in my second semester I changed my major to Fashion Design. It amazed me that I could create something tangible that represented me. I learned how to create a garment, from sketching the idea to the actual construction of it. I began sewing my own outfits to wear to campus parties. Who would have known? I took a range of courses from public speaking to art history, illustration, to communications, so that I could get as much as I could get from college. The second semester Talia and I also moved from main campus to south campus, where the upper classmen lived: 201 Winding Ridge is where we experienced so many great things. That's where I created my first garments, met my special friend the Illustrious "Lus" Greatmind Salley (his family belong to the Five Percent Nation), reunited with Clarence Cannon, threw a huge cookout to show the members of Alpha Kappa Alpha Sorority Inc. we were interested in joining, and also became a member of AKA.

JAI HUDSON

ALPHA KAPPA ALPHA SORORITY INC.

My sophomore year at SU, I pledged twice to become a member of Alpha Kappa Alpha Inc. The Iota Upsilon chapter of AKA at SU was not active at that time. There weren't any undergrad AKAs to keep the sororities presence alive on campus. That's what we wanted to change. The only way to bring AKA back to SU was to pledge so that the undergraduate chapter would be active again. That was one of the most influential events in my life. Those experiences taught me humility, sisterhood, and to never give up. When we were in high school, Talia and the seniors Tamara Carter and Latoya Gatlin at HSTAT, created a junior sorority called Gamma Phi Si. They put on step shows, had t-shirts made with the logo and even had a chant. So we had a little preparation and that started my interest in sororities.

JAI HUDSON

Talia and I first pledged at a nearby school named Oswego College. We met an AKA that lived in Syracuse New York named Cortina. She was super cool and welcomed Talia and me to Syracuse. She took us around and introduced us to other AKA women. She even connected us with the AKAs at Oswego. They would help us by pledging us so that we could bring AKA back to SU. We started in the fall of 1997. I was number one on line and Talia was number two.

I couldn't believe Talia and I were cross pledging to bring AKA back to Syracuse University's campus. We were driving from SU to Oswego every night after class. If you have ever heard about Syracuse, NY weather in the winter, then you know the snow is very bad. Talia's car swerved on the highway several times and we even experienced a tornado in our travels to

Oswego. Four girls conducted the AKA chapter at Oswego. They pledged us for six weeks until the line was dropped. I won't go into why it ended, however I will say Oswego's chapter was threatened. I will always appreciate and respect the four women from Oswego that taught us the true meaning of sisterhood. Crazy thing was that one of the AKAs that pledged us was named Jaquetta. How ironic! I learned so much from them. They also created a process that was so beneficial. Talia and I protected each other. I also learned how to multitask, how to run a chapter, and the positive process of crossing the burning sands.

Hazing is illegal and is a crime, but Pledging is legal. The lines get blurred sometimes. However, if you know the history of black sororities, pledging is a process that happens with the intention of learning the true meaning of sisterhood. It was created to

unite Black students on college campuses.
1908 was the year when the first Black
Greek Sorority was created — Alpha Kappa
Alpha Sorority Incorporated. Back then,
racism was common on college campuses.
Organizations like AKA and Alpha Phi Alpha,
DST, Omega Psi Phi, etc. created a platform
for students to unite in sisterhood and
service. But some members get out of
control with power. Some "big sisters and
brothers" abuse their power and it becomes
more about humiliation from a pain and loss
perspective rather than teaching humility
from a gain perspective. To be humble is a
benefit, a blessing, and a positive. However,
tearing someone down to make them feel
less than because you want more power is
when the organization strays from the ideals
AKA was founded on. Because of this, they
spoil it for the rest of us. That's when the

JAI HUDSON

lines can become blurred between pledging and hazing.

New members crossing over to Alpha Kappa Alpha Sorority Incorporated are closely watched. So after the Oswego line was dropped, Talia and I found a soror in the grad school at SU willing to pledge us so we could finish the process we started. The second time we pledged, we met other girls who were interested in AKA also. So there were now 10 girls on my line. It was different from the first line I was on. This time instead of having to be accountable for one person, Talia, I now had nine other girls to connect with. There were so many times I wanted to drop or give up. My grades were slipping and it was so hard to stay on top of everything.

Pledging is a very difficult experience. It teaches you how to balance. When I was pledging to become a member of AKA, I had to balance my demanding schedule at school while staying on top of information I was taught about AKA. When we crossed, we were able to bring AKA Sorority Inc. back to Syracuse University's campus. It had been years since AKA had a presence on campus. It felt so good. AKA was the first black sorority created at Howard University to unite minority women. Maya Angelou, Phylicia Rashad, Alice Walker, Iyanla Vanzant, and so on, were all famous AKAs that I looked up to. Now we were members. We became even more popular on campus. I remember how amazing it felt to lead my sisters' line strolling at the parties to the powerful song "Victory" by Puff Daddy and BIG while wearing the clothes I created. It was such an indescribable feeling. I felt powerful, seen, and valued.

So, my college years were great. I had so many great experiences. I gained new

sisters of Alpha Kappa Alpha Sorority Inc., I
was creating clothes, driving to other schools
to make the SU AKA presence felt, shutting
down Temple University Greek fest, strolling
or party walking at the Greek parties, and
just being on my own. I experienced a lot of
great things at Syracuse University. Those
are memories I will never forget. After
college Talia worked in NYC but received a
job in LA. She was now producing for
television. I visited LA and stayed in her
apartment in *Brentwood, CA.* She invited
me out to see if LA would be the place I
began my journey. Los Angeles was a
beautiful experience, however something
was calling me back in New York City. It
was time to stand on my own and start my
life. The possibilities were endless. So I
went to live in Flatbush Brooklyn NY with my
childhood friend Clarence Cannon.

"VICTORY"

Song by Puff Daddy and Notorious BIG & Busta Rhymes

Yo the sun don't shine forever
But as long as it's here
Then we might as well shine together
Better now than never
Business before pleasure
P-diddy and the fam,
Who you know do it better?
Yeah right, no matter what, we air tight
So when you hear somethin,
Make sure you hear it right
Don't make a ass outta yourself,
By assuming
Our music keeps you movin,
What are you provin?
You know that I'm two levels
Above you baby
Hug me baby, imma make you love me baby
Talking crazy ain't gonna
Get you nothing but choked
And that jealousy is only
Gonna leave you broke
So the only thing left now
is God for these cats
And Big you know you
Too hard for these cats
I'm a win cause I'm

JAI HUDSON

Too smart for these cats
While they making up facts (uhh)
You raking up plaques

JAI HUDSON

VIII
DREAMS DO COME TRUE

"DREAMS"

Song by Jay Z, featuring Notorious Big, and Faith Evans

Had A Dream I Said
About Big I Said....

I see I said
Jealousy I said
Got the whole industry mad at me I said
BI said Hov remind yourself
Nobody built like you, you designed yourself
I agree I said my one of kind self
Get stoned everyday like Jesus did
What he said, I said had been said before
Keep doing your thing he said
Say no more

IT WAS ALL A DREAM

In my teens I avoided emotions and my true feelings. My 20s was pretty much the same. Emotions surfaced but I ran away from them. I did not want to deal with things. If the emotion was regarding my mother, I usually retreated or closed my heart. If the situation was with a relationship, isolation or break-up was usually the outcome. I would not let myself feel deeply for anyone again.

When I lived in Flatbush Brooklyn "Parkside" I had new friends and roommates who were all males. During my last year of college I was reunited with my middle school friend Clarence Cannon. After college I went to live with Clarence and his two roommates. We lived on the 4th floor of a high-rise apartment building over looking Prospect Park. Clarence had been rooming with Richard and Emanuel. They were all in their 20s working in New York City. It was such a beautiful environment for me. We were all motivated individuals taking chances. I was also able to be around male peers who didn't want anything sexually from me. They loved that I was the only female around all them. I guess I balanced the environment. I was super motivated to reach my goals. I had guys like Emanuel, Richard, Clarence, The Milan's, etc. who were modeling making your dreams reality.

Because I was so different growing up, the black sheep of the family, it felt great to be around others who shared some of the same experiences I did. We developed a crew or family of like-minded individuals in NYC. We called ourselves the Hotboyz.

The creation happened very organically. We threw some major house parties right inside of our Parkside apt. An event that started out as a small party celebrating Clarence and my birthday, May 21st & May

22nd, in our Parkside living room quickly became a weekly party at a major club in NYC. We travelled to other states, spreading our brand all over the U.S. The parties and brand that Hotboyz created was different than what was happening in NYC. The Hotboyz were attractive men in New York City, working in music, film, TV, public relations, marketing, etc. We were living our dreams and having fun doing it.

Some of the Hotboyz experienced abuse also, and I started to realize that abuse was common and almost always dealt with the same way. We became outlets for one another. We could relate and talk about the pain. We could dream and be as creative as we wanted. There was so much music, fashion, art, and inspiration all around. It was a creative playground for me. I spoke to my mother via phone from time to time. She seemed interested in the life I was living.

JAI HUDSON

Now that I look back, I can see how my life looked similar to my mom's: she was the only female amongst all her brothers and now I was the only female within a crew of guys.

For a long time I never wanted to be like my mom. I would never let a man control me like that. I would always maintain my health and physique. But that wasn't all my mother was, that was just one part of her. She had great qualities too. Somehow I was starting to develop some qualities I admired about my mother. I admired the fact that she cared deeply about people. She loved to smile. Although my mom didn't know how to be emotionally available for me, she'd send me money from time to time, helping me when I fell short financially.

I didn't take the typical 9 to 5 city job. Art has always been my passion. If you know anything about that life then you know the term "starving artist." We don't have health benefits and a weekly paycheck as most city jobs do. There's no real stability when you are an artist. However, this was my gift. This way of survival teaches you to discover your gift and believe in yourself. Within the creative field, your gift tends to be how you pay the bills. So belief in self is very important and necessary.

My mom always made sure that I was OK. She also listened to all my problems and I could be vulnerable with her. I could cry, I could tell her I didn't feel good enough, and she'd help me see why I was enough. I could ask her for money and not feel like I've failed. I could tell her I didn't want to live any more because it got extremely difficult and she'd show me how I had so much to live for. Even if she couldn't be there emotionally in the way I needed, she was there in her own way, judgment free. She understood me. She always listened to me. She was my soft place to fall. Our relationship was changing and I tried very hard to let go of all the baggage I had about the past.

MAYBE NEXT TIME

I started to develop a strong desire to see my father. I guess emotions were starting to resurface again and I wanted to see the guy I looked so much like. So I decided to talk with my grandmother, his mother, about it. Of course, she warned me ahead of time. My grandmother asked me if I was sure this was something I wanted to do. My father, Ricky Washington, was born on November 7th and suffers from schizophrenia. My grandmother told me that after I was born, he wanted so bad to provide for my mother and me. He wanted to be a good father and a great man to my mother.

JAI HUDSON

But things began to change. He started to develop symptoms and he couldn't see how the people around him were affected. When my mom experienced these changes, she tried to get away. She didn't want to be with him anymore and that crushed him. That hurt my father so deeply. Around the same time my grandmother, his mother, was beaten and raped. All of these events affected my father tremendously. Mentally, my father has never been the same. My grandmother warned me to not have expectations regarding my dad. She didn't want me to get hurt. Still, this was something I wanted to do. I don't know why it was so important, but I needed to see him.

My grandmother gave me his number and I decided to call. I didn't know if it was a good or bad idea, I really didn't think about that. This was my father and I was determined to know him. When I called, I heard that voice that I remembered as a child calling for me to come out of hiding. No one else sounded like my father. He was happy to hear my voice also. He said so. I told him that I was about to go on tour with 50 Cent, I told him about my friends, I told him I was a fashion stylist, and I told him how life was for me presently. I couldn't believe I was speaking to the man who created me. My father. I even went to see him. I took "Lus" with me. Lus became a special friend to me.

We started to talk more over the phone too. However, most conversations ended the same way. It was like a light suddenly switched off. Every time we spoke he would have to ask, "How's your mother?" That was such a tricky question because no matter how I answered it the conversation ended badly. The conversation immediately went downhill from there. Everything resulted in

how my mom did him wrong. How my
mother was the worst person on the face of
the earth and caused him so much pain. I
didn't want to hear this. I had heard so much
negativity in the past about him. Now I was
hearing negativity about her. It was constant
"Donna bashing." This made me feel so lost.
I was attempting to have a connection with
the man who created me.

I couldn't understand what was up with
my parents; did they ever really like each
other? I didn't want to be caught in this
negative web created by both my mother
and father. I wasn't in their relationship in
that way. I don't know who did what and why
my mother left him. My intention in calling
him was to get to know my dad. I wanted to
get to know *the other part of me.* I wanted to
learn about me. His conversations let me
know that now wasn't the time. *Better luck
next time.*

JAI HUDSON

MY TALENTS

I worked at Calvin Klein, Issey Miyake, Columbia Records, King Magazine, and eventually with the fashion stylist Misa Hylton. I also went after my dreams of working in music. After interning in 2000 at Columbia Records, I decided I wanted to be part of the creative process of a music artist career. I saw how the promotions department handled the radio DJs and street teams, then the A&R's scouting new artists, producers and music, and then finally the marketing department. This area of music drew me in. It dealt with how you package up an artist and sell to the consumer. Marketing always stood out to me, because that department dealt with the creativity and image of the artist.

That led me to designing and constructing clothing for artists, models, and actresses. I remember working with a stylist named Seannita Palmer in which I received the opportunity to create clothing for the girls in Jay Z's H to the IZZO video. During this time, customizing clothing was the trend and I was creating right along with it. So The Roc supplied us with Rocawear t-shirts and I added net fabric, zippers, gathers, leather, etc. I created each shirt with a different design. When I saw the work I did in the video I was on a cloud higher than nine! How about 9999? Then from that job, I received the opportunity to create something for one of my favorite artists, Aaliyah. Music and fashion companies like Rocawear, Badboy/Sean John, Babyphat were dominating the culture at this time.

In 1999 there was a celebrity baseball game — Rocawear vs. Badboy in the Hamptons. Rocawear hired us to create shirts again for the players on the team. Aaliyah was one of the main players. I don't even remember who won the game. I couldn't get over the fact that Aaliyah was wearing a shirt I created. This was truly a dream come true: it showed me that dreams do come true. Aaliyah was someone I respected as a true artist. I had posters up of her. Now I was creating clothing that she wore!

August 25 2001, we lost an angel: Aaliyah Haughton. She was such an inspiration to me. She showed me that being a tomboy was still beautiful and that having a good heart is what truly matters. Her passing affected me. We were the same age. So, seeing 1979 – August 25, 2001 next to her name was a major wake-up call. Life is super precious and not promised. Aaliyah Haughton, our Angel, you will always be missed.

At this time I was still working with Seannita Parmer. Seannita was hired at

King magazine as the fashion editor. That's where I met Datwon Thomas. He created King magazine and is overall a great spirit to the world. We were creating some of the most amazing custom pieces and styling the celebrities being featured in the magazine.

Simultaneously I was being exposed to music with my friend Jane Blaze. She was the first person I met that was signed to a major record label — Jive Records. I started to attend her studio sessions and accompany her to label meetings. She was such an incredible artist. She rapped, she sang, played instruments, and even produced. Jane exposed me to different artists and producers in the music industry.

NINE ELEVEN – 9/11

On the night of September 10th I was sewing up some last-minute clothing at Seannita's apartment in Tribeca. My friend William

Cooley was with Camille and I. Camille was from LA and was interning with us. We decided to sleep over and head back to Brooklyn in the morning. At 8am, I woke Will up so that we could head out. I remember looking at my phone at 8:22am before going down into the train station. When we reached the Parkside Station, we went upstairs to our apartment to find Rich watching the news. We quickly gathered in front of the television. We watched the replay of a plane crashing into the World Trade Tower.

This was devastating. I couldn't believe this was happening right down the block from where Will and I just came from. Then suddenly, from the corner of the screen another plane crashed into the second tower. First I thought it was an instant replay, but then I realized this was no accident. Both towers were now on fire. I immediately called my mother who worked down the block from the World Trade Center at 100 Gold Street. She answered the phone and told me she was walking over the Brooklyn Bridge to Brooklyn because the trains were shut down. I couldn't believe what was happening. The twin towers were the tallest buildings in the U.S. Now the towers were under attack. New York City was under attack.

I remember thinking *I hope this isn't* the end *that I heard people talked about.* Then on the news they showed other planes crashing into the capitol and one disappearing in the air. What was happening to the United States? Then suddenly the first tower collapsed. There were people still trapped inside. People were jumping out of the windows trying to escape the heat of the fire. This seemed like a scene in a movie or even a nightmare. Then the second tower came down. All I could think about was all

JAI HUDSON

the lives that were lost. The Twin Towers of New York City were deleted from the skyline. It was truly unbelievable.

WORLD TOUR

In 2002 I went to work for Misa Hylton at her company Chyna Doll Enterprises. She was responsible for developing the image and style for Mary J Blige, Lil Kim, Jodeci, Kimora — she is a major part of the style creation for the Badboy movement. One day I was watching an awards show and saw Lil Kim performing. She came out in a pink convertible "Barbie" car, dressed in a cropped top and denim jeans that were custom-designed. This was the first time I had seen something like that done in that way. Lil' Kim was more of a provocative artist. She is very feminine and used sex as her weapon of choice. So, to see her in jeans and timberland construction boots was mind-blowing for me. I knew that style had been created by Misa Hylton. She was Lil' Kim's stylist. Misa was incredible to me- everything about her. Her style- *colorful furs and wigs, large diamonds, jerseys and combat boots, blonde hair, head to toe Fendi suits.... Simply put it was MAJOR!* She was showcasing a lifestyle that was so rich yet authentic. When I saw all she was creating, I knew that I wanted to work with her. And like magic I received the opportunity to study from a great like Misa. Chyna Doll Ent. was such an amazing place to grow and learn the styling game. I was around one of the major *style-contributors* to the Badboy Movement. I was assisting Misa, styling major entertainers such as Queen Latifah, Lil Kim, Mary J Blige, 50 Cent and G-Unit, Kimora Lee Simmons, Missy Elliott, and so many others. I was around some amazing individuals at Chyna Doll- Misa, Tiffany,

Trena, Tiana, Reka, Wouri, Clarence, Jay, Aaron, Mariel Haen, Groovey Lew, and Bharat. I learned *to always stay true to what you do because that's a gift In itself. "No one can do what I can do," words from Misa Hylton-I will never forget.*

April 25, 2002 we lost another creative force within popular music. Lisa "Left Eye" Lopes, the rapper of the female group TLC, was killed in a car crash in Honduras. Left Eye was so special to me. When TLC came out I felt like finally there were girls just like me. They were promoting girl power, addressing tough social issues and doing this all while dressing in oversized and baggy clothing. The TLC movement taught me to stand in my power and be grateful for how God had created me, tomboy and all. Thank you TLC and Left Eye.

I left July 5, 2005 on the 50 Cent and Eminem Massacre tour. We flew straight to

Venice Italy for the first show of the tour. I
was now a fashion stylist working for Chyna
Doll Enterprises with Misa Hylton. I learned a
lot from Misa being on tour. I also had to
step up professionally on tour. Misa had
small kids in school that year so she allowed
me to travel on the European tour in
representation of her.   That was big!

Venice is such a beautiful place. *Wow* is
all I can say. It is one of the most magical
places I've ever been. Picture this: no
streets, just water. No cars, just boats. So
let's say you dropped something out of your
window by accident, you're basically going
swimming to retrieve it. Seriously. We also
travelled to London, Paris, Italy, Amsterdam,
Milan, Rome, Germany, Florence,
Switzerland, and South of France. The view
from my window in the South of France was
like an endless blue ocean. It was like the
sky and the ocean connected. It's such a

vision to see. Travelling to these different countries was incredible. We were riding on private planes, at the best hotels, travelling in so much style. It was such an incredible way to experience overseas for the first time. How blessed was I? From shopping in Paris, shooting Hustler Ambition music video in the heart of London, police escorts from the venue to the sold-out after-parties, and receiving special treatment because you're with a major artist — 50 Cent was huge. Who would have ever thought a girl from the Bedford Stuyvesant Brooklyn, Brevoort projects could be walking the streets of Paris? Who would have ever thought I would be living aspects of my dreams at this point in my life? The feeling was so intoxicating.

"SKY'S THE LIMIT"

Song by Notorious Big

Sky is the limit and you know that you keep on
just keep on pressin on
Sky is the limit and you know that you can have
What you want, pressin what you want
Sky is the limit and you know that you keep on
Just keep on pressin on
sky is the limit and you know that you can have
What you want, be what you want, have what you
want, be what you want

FINDING MY POWER

When I returned home I was so inspired. After seeing the world and being inspired by the Chyna Doll Ent. family, I knew that even the sky wasn't the limit. I came home and decided to develop a team. My boy Dion was styling at the time so I decided to join forces with him. We were styling Trey Songz, Donnell Jones, several new artists signed to Universal, and now Pharrell's new rap duo, The Clipse.

My friend Keith Wooten who was working at Jive Records at the time thought we would be great stylists for the Clipse. So I created a storybook of inspiration that included images of the 90s street style in Harlem NY. *Paid n Full, dope dealers, cars, fashion, money, the fast life* was the theme they wanted to portray. I remember talking to Pusha T from The Clipse on the phone and passionately explaining the direction we expressed in the

storyboard. Dion was from Harlem NY and I
had been living in Harlem ever since 2004. I
loved the whole style element from Harlem.
It was rich, it was regal, and it was flashy.
Pusha T loved my ideas and hired us to style
The Clipse for their upcoming projects. I
remember the first time I met Pharrell. He
walked into the "Mr. Me Too" video styling
room and introduced himself to me. Pharrell
has this air about him. He made me feel like
he was a real person, no different than me.
He came straight to the clothing rack and
asked if he could look.

I watched his expressions to see if he
liked the clothing we pulled and created for
the Clipse. He really got into the aesthetics
and details of the clothing. Then he looked at
the sneakers, the rope chains, Gucci link
chains, gazelles, Sergio Tacchini style
polo's, hard denim levis, Ralph Lauren
mixed with Gucci, Dapper Dan and 5001

JAI HUDSON

Flavors inspired baseball style jackets, etc. It was an overload of every element that consisted of that time in Harlem. He shook his head with approval of the creative direction and overall style of the clothes. He said, "You're dope." I was the only one in the styling area at this time because Dion was on set with the Clipse shooting a scene in their *Mr. Me Too* music video. Wow! Pharrell thought we were dope. Then he started talking to me. Asking my opinion on different things. He then started to talk about a new line of clothing he was developing. He was so excited. I recognized that enthusiasm — I had the same excitement about creating. I will never forget that moment. Thank you Pharrell.

I shared an apartment with Walter Steele Jr. We met in 2001 at our Parkside apt. We connected instantly. Walter was a dancer who danced for several music acts. The oldest of nine brothers and sisters, he was born and raised in the Bronx. Walter and I were both super passionate about music and artistry. We connected creatively; it was like he was my creative soul twin.

Walter and I decided we were going to develop a singing group inspired by TLC and Salt-N-Pepa. We created online posts on MySpace and even created flyers. We were determined to make our ideas come to life. One day after a Clipse shoot, Walter, Dion and I were unloading wardrobe back into my apartment. After we took the last load up, Dion called me to come back downstairs to see something. I was a little hesitant because it had started to rain. But Walter insisted. So I went downstairs and experienced something that would change my world completely.

I walked over to the telephone post where Dion and Walter were standing. I could see that a young girl was with them and was hiding under a burgundy hoody. Dion said, "Jai she can sing — you have to hear her." So I asked her to sing something for me. This small-framed girl opened her mouth to sing and shocked me completely. She sang "I Need You Baby," by Lauryn Hill. I couldn't believe what I was hearing. She had the tone of voice I've always loved and connected to. It was raspy, soulful yet rebellious, but soothing at the same time. Her voice gave me the chills. I kept a poker face however, and asked her to sing something else. I wanted to hear her range. She then sang the gospel song "His Eyes on the Sparrow." I was blown away. And she sang two songs Lauryn Hill famously sang. *We had found her! My muse, my secret weapon, and the lead singer of our girl group.* Her name was Teyana Taylor.

JAI HUDSON

Soon after that auspicious meeting the
group quickly formed. It consisted of Teyana,
Brionne (the rapper of the group, and
Diamond, who was the softer vocalist (my
friend Reemo's daughter). The group was
complete. Dice was in full effect. We started
rehearsals, wrote songs, and I tried to
nurture them so they knew the importance of
hard work and commitment. I wanted them
to see that if they believed in themselves
more than I believed in them, they could
achieve anything they wanted.

STARTRAK

After a few months of development, we
realized that Teyana was ready for the
world. She had been training ever since she
was young. So, Teyana decided to go solo
and we decided to find a replacement for the
group. Because I had been working with the
Clipse and Pharrell, and Teyana connected

so much with the Startrak movement, it seemed like a no-brainer. So by the grace of God, and a lot of persuasion my friend Rahlo (who was working at Universal Records) scheduled a meeting with Kevin Law. Kevin had a close connection with Pharrell on the music side.

When I told Teyana we had the meeting, she was so happy. I remember it was a Friday and the meeting was at the Four Seasons on 57th Street in Manhattan. We waited into the lobby with so much anticipation. If Teyana ever says she wasn't nervous, she's lying. Suddenly, Pharrell walked up with Yanley Arty and greeted us. Pharrell looked at me with disbelief — he was surprised to see me, and excited when he realized the connection. We followed him upstairs to his hotel room and took a seat. There was some small talk for about two minutes. Then Teyana began to sing. I believe she sang about three or four songs before he stopped her. There was a very short silence, then Pharrell spoke. "I want to sign you right now. Are you interested?" Teyana replied, "Yes!" Of course Teyana wanted to be a part of Startrak music. That was a dream of hers and now it was becoming reality.

After the meeting with Pharrell, Jimmy Iovine and Pharrell flew us out to Los Angeles so Teyana could sing for the label execs. She serenaded them and now these powerful men in music were on board as well. We were sitting in a room in Interscope Records in Los Angeles with these important execs that have changed several artist's careers. Now our lives would change forever.

After Teyana got her deal we wanted to keep the momentum going so we decided to have her Sweet 16 on MTV's "My Super

Sweet 16" show. It was a huge success.
Now the world knew who Teyana Taylor
was. Following the party, the label was ready
to see the direction of Teyana's image. They
needed to know how they would present her
to the world. This was what I did. I had been
developing Teyana for the past two years. I
created storyboards in 3.5 seconds. Yes, I'm
exaggerating, but this was "my baby," my
project I had nurtured, prayed on,
strategized to bring to life, so this was
second nature to me. I created the
storyboards, presented them to Teyana's
mother Nikki Taylor, and she took them to
Yanley Arty at Startrak. They told me that
Yanley loved it. I was so excited and
confident in what I had created.

Dion, Walter and I went straight to work
to find clothing that helped us achieve
Teyana's image. A day before the first shoot,
Nikki called me with some disturbing news.

JAI HUDSON

She gave me the impression that the label didn't think it was a good idea for me to come to the shoot. I couldn't believe what I was hearing. So they wanted my ideas and clothes but not me? Why did she feel this way? I felt so low. I could have said "F-it" and gone anyway. However, something told me to move on. I didn't want to be somewhere I wasn't wanted. So I gracefully threw in the towel. I had heard stories of how when artists get signed, the people who made sacrifices for them to get signed usually are left behind. I was just following my heart concerning Teyana. I didn't get contracts signed by Teyana, so my involvement wasn't guaranteed. A lesson I had to learn early on in the business.

There were a few shady occurrences before this particular incident, but I didn't feel like fighting to be part of something that obviously didn't want me to be a part of it. So

when I made the decision to not go further, I
didn't want to hinder any part of Teyana's
career. That's just not the person I am.
Besides, what did I want? Compensation? I
felt like money couldn't make up for the fact
that my presence was not wanted. I didn't
want to mess up the vibes with her new
label. This was her dream. It wasn't the
success that I imagined. My manifestations
wouldn't happen with such yucky feelings
attached. My success would feel good, and
exactly how it feels when I'm dreaming of it. I
was part of Teyana's life in the moments she
needed me and vice versa. Being part of her
story in that way let me know I did have a
power. I am destined for greatness. Look
what I was able to create with limited tools
and understanding. I had a gift.

I'm so proud of Teyana and all she has
accomplished and has become. I saw it in
her. So when I listened to her first album

titled "7" (completion for some and Symbolism of God for me), I cried with joy and happiness. She manifested her dreams.

I had some great experiences and relationships where I learned a lot about myself. I had gone through my share of ups and downs, but for the most part I loved who I was becoming. Travelling, relationships, creating, great friendships, music, and just living life each day as it happened was my life. I always wondered, if I had stayed in my house back in Queens, would I have experienced such great things? All I know for sure is that I felt truly blessed.

JAI HUDSON

"SORRY"

Song by Teyana Taylor

He tells me I'm beautiful
Every day
The better part of him hear him say
Now as you watch from far away
All I can say
I'm so sorry
You had you cake and a gift that day
Something that our love didn't create
Now as you watch from far away all I can say
I'm so sorry
Never again cause I know
Just what it means to love and be loved
Now as you watch from far away
All I can say is
I'm so sorry
I'm sorry you didn't know how to love me
I'm sorry I wasn't beautiful to you

IX

THE BEGINNING

OF THE BEGINNING

"LIKE A SIMMONS WHIPPIN' PASTRY"

In 2009, I worked as the marketing and creative brand manager at Pastry (a sneaker brand), founded by Angela and Vanessa Simmons I was in heaven. Not only was I making important brand decisions but I received the opportunity to work with my dear friend Kim Snow. I met Kim back when I was at Chyna Doll Entertainment. She worked at Mecca then Ecko brands. As a stylist, PR people at clothing lines become our best friends. We need each other. They allow us to borrow their brand and we put their product on celebrities — which equals sales for them.

So I was working for Kim now, someone I had so much respect and admiration for. We were a great team. We were bringing "the cool factor" to the Pastry Brand. Because of my huge interest in sneakers and because I had been an athlete, this was right up my alley. We developed a concert directly helping to drive sales to the malls. We called the tour "Pastry Rocks The Mall," with headliner Keri Hilson, as well as upcoming artists in each town. We had appearances by Trina, and hosted by Angela and Vanessa Simmons. It was so amazing putting on these mini concerts. Kim and I handled the booking of artists, transportation, radio promotions, production of the show, clothing for models, all affiliation and contracts-it was so much we were learning. We were a marketing power team.

We exposed the brand to so much "cool" factor that even Jay Z put Pastry in the NYC anthem "Empire State of Mind," featuring Alicia Keys. "Catch me in the kitchen like a Simmons whipping Pastry." This is truly what it means to have a natural high. We were so naturally high because we contributed to the success of a brand we really believed in. Not to mention Kim and I loved Jay Z, he is one of our favorite artists. It was an epic moment.

"EMPIRE STATE OF MIND"

Song by JAY Z and ALICIA KEYS

Yeah I'm out that Brooklyn,
Now I'm down in Tribeca
Right next to Deniro,
But I'll be hood forever
I'm the new Sinatra,
And since I made it here
I can make it anywhere, yeah,
They love me everywhere
I used to cop in Harlem,
All of my Dominicanos
Right there up on Broadway,
Pull me back to that McDonald's
Took it to my stash spot, 560 State Street
Catch me in the kitchen like the Simmons'
whipping pastry
[chorus — Alicia keys:]
New york, concrete jungle
Where dreams are made of
There's nothin' you can't do
Now you're in new york
These streets will make you
Feel brand new
The lights will inspire you
Let's hear it for new york,
New york, new york
[bridge — Alicia keys:]

JAI HUDSON

One hand in the air for the big city
Street lights, big dreams, all lookin' pretty
No place in the world that could compare
Put your lighters in the air
Everybody say "yeah, yeah, yeah, yeah" (c'mon,
c'mon)
I'm from...

JAI HUDSON

CATCHING UP

Now in my 30s, it became difficult to run from the past. In my relationships I began to recognize an emotional disability. I couldn't give myself whole-heartedly and didn't allow myself to receive love either. I was giving, giving, giving, but not filling up with anything. So I was depleted internally because I was empty from the start.

One day after work I was at home preparing for the next day when I received a call from my sister. She was at my mother's house and said my mom didn't look well. I asked her to put my mom on the phone. She didn't sound like my mom, and her responses were incomprehensible. One of my friends named Jamie who worked in a hospital was at my house, and hearing what was happening with my mom. The fact that she was slurring her speech, reminded him

of a certain sickness. He told me to have her
hold something in her hands. So I told my
sister to have her hold an object in her left
hand. My sister responded saying my mom
couldn't do it. Then my friend said, have her
write her name. So I told my sister. Again
she couldn't perform the task. I told my
friend what my sister observed and his
response was "I think she's having a stroke."
I immediately had my friend call an
ambulance while I continued to talk to my
sister. I told her to tell my mother to get
ready to go to the hospital. I knew she would
not want to go, however I really didn't care
what she wanted to do at this point. My
mother really disliked hospitals. But she was
going and I was adamant about that.

I heard a male's voice in the background
and I asked who that was. My sister
responded that it was her father (country). I
asked what were they doing when she got

there. She said they were lying in bed watching a movie. Wait a minute! I know I didn't just hear that correctly. She was experiencing a stroke while in the bed with her husband? And he did nothing? How could you lay with her and not know something is wrong? So, if my sister didn't go over to my mother's house and realize something was wrong, this situation could have been much worse. I was in Harlem and yet I was the one who had to call an ambulance to pick her up in Brooklyn and take her to the hospital? Not her husband who was lying right beside her? This was just incredible to me. I was so confused.

My mom didn't like hospitals, and put up a fight of course — she wouldn't be my mom if she didn't. The ambulance arrived and confirmed that she needed to go to the hospital. My mom was spaced out, according to my sister. She was definitely

having a stroke. I met my mom at the
hospital. She didn't look good at all— pale,
frail, and not as strong as she usually was. I
found out she had a septic stroke, which is
related to diabetes. She had diabetes and
didn't tell me. I think she didn't want me to
worry. But I wish she had said something to
me. She was in ICU and lost almost half her
body weight. I couldn't believe this was
happening.

She was in the hospital close to two
months. I was there almost every day and
when she came home I went with her to
most of her doctor appointments. She was
starting to develop a tingling sensation in her
feet and it became painful to walk. She was
losing the feeling in her legs. These were the
same legs that raced me as a child, the
same legs that carried her over the Brooklyn
Bridge when we walked to Brooklyn from her
job. I couldn't believe this was happening to

my mother. My mom was super strong. That's where I got my strength. So to see my mom losing her ability to walk, was really deep for me. My mother was a warrior.

I was certified as a personal trainer and I was determined to help her regain her strength. I went to her physical therapy and neurology appointments. I did research of my own as well. She told me she had sciatica so I was determined to figure out something she could do to help with pain. I told her about yoga and explained that it could help with healing. She now had to walk with a cane and ride in access-a-ride car service to work. When I went to see her at work, it was so difficult watching her in pain as she walked to embrace me. My mom's legs were deteriorating. I could see the pain in her eyes. As much as I tried to give her remedies and suggestions I couldn't force

JAI HUDSON

her to do the work. She had to do it for
herself. She had to want to get better.

X

HISTORY REPEATS ITSELF

JAI HUDSON

"DOUBT"

Song By Mary j Blige

You said I'd never be a leader
You said I'd never wear a crown
If I wanted to be someone
I should learn to settle down
(you should know better)
I tell myself (you'll never go further)
I warn myself (you'll never be better)
Don't know me that well
I made it to the end I nearly paid the cost
I lost a lot of friends I sacrificed a lot
I'd do it all again 'cause I made it to the top
But I can't keep doubting myself anymore
No! I can't keep doubting myself
Now you're looking at a leader
Now you're staring at a queen
You said I'll never be someone
But now I'm pulling all the strings

FORGET THE PAST?

In the midst of my own forgetting of the past, I often wondered how my mother felt about what happened. What were her worries? What happened to her as a child? A person is as good as the teachings they received. She did what she knew. I always wondered how she could stay with a man like country. Eventually I learned that when you know better, you do better.

"Psychologically, there are few things as upsetting as imagining that your husband is the kind of man who would sexually abuse a child. While the pedophile often feels little guilt, anxiety, or remorse about their own behavior, the wives feel significant anxiety but use denial and rationalization to sweep their suspicions under the rug. They don't focus on the feelings of the victim because all their energy goes into feeling sorry for themselves because they made a mistake in choosing the wrong man to marry. The wives of pedophiles rarely admit to others that they knew or suspected what was going on, but these are their thoughts and fears in their most dark and private moments. Above all, why these women don't come forward or even admit the problem to themselves for more than a minute or two is that they don't want their husband to get in trouble with the law, because this would call attention to the women by their sides and make the women look guilty, too, for standing by all along as the child gets abused." – Seth Meyers, PsyD. Psychology Today, "Insight is 20/20"

The second time I saw my mother cry was when I tried to open up and talk to her about my abuse. I had to be about 26 or 28 years old. This was one of the times when *the* feelings resurfaced again. I started the conversation and began to tell her how I felt.

I expressed how being abused made me feel. My mom stopped me abruptly by saying, "Jacquetta, it happened to me too." And she started to cry. I immediately stopped expressing my feelings, closed up, and tried to console her — giving her the attention I so desperately wanted. She didn't know how to console me. I later found out that two family members who are now deceased sexually abused my mom. I tried to think of how she must have felt. Was she raped? Did she tell anyone? This explained a lot. She couldn't save me because no one saved her.

My mother's generation was taught to keep quiet regarding family matters. I can totally see my mom suffering from sexual abuse as well. Knowing her, she didn't tell anyone, I felt my mother's pain. I wish someone could have protected her. I wish someone could have saved her. No one

JAI HUDSON

protected her so how could she know how to protect me? Imagine the holes she developed in her growth From experience I know firsthand that low self-esteem develops. If no one noticed something was wrong, she may have felt not good enough too. Then did she attach the uncomfortable feelings towards the abuser to other males? Was she just like me?

When a person is exposed to sexuality too early in age, it affects their emotional relationships heavily. When my mom met country, he was super attentive, catering and extremely into her — she was swept off her feet. Her immediate needs were being met. So the holes of low self-esteem and unworthiness my mom suffered were filled by country. Sometimes it's difficult to see the deep dark things wrong with a person when your holes are being met temporarily. My mom was broken. Look at how my family dealt with my mother's sister. They didn't deal with it at all. And because of that, my mom most likely felt that her abuse wasn't something important enough to be dealt with either. She was taught at a young age to keep quiet about family matters — and about her own pain.

History repeated itself when it came to my mother suffering from sexual abuse. Who knows what happened to others in the family before her. It was a cycle, that by the grace of God, I was able to disconnect from. I experienced abuse, yes. However, that tradition of not dealing with it, not speaking up about it and allowing my circumstances to define my future, was not part of my personality or belief system. I wanted more. But imagine how many individuals get caught within a cycle of dysfunctions established by the generations before them. The belief system is embedded within us.

JAI HUDSON

We conduct our lives with the ideals of our parents, and so on. History does not have to repeat itself: the cycle *can* be broken. I had to recognize that God had made me different, unique, and that I could break the cycle. I had a purpose and I was ready to heal so I could find out what my purpose was.

"BAG LADY"
Song by Erykah Badu

Bag lady you gone hurt your back
Dragging all them bags like that
I guess nobody ever told you
All you must hold onto, is you, is you, is you
One day all them bags gon' get in your way
One day all them bags gon' get in your way
I said one day all them bags gon' get in your way
One day all them bags gon' get in your way, so pack
light,
Pack light, mm, pack light, pack light, oh ooh
Bag lady you gon' miss your bus
You can't hurry up, 'cause you got too much stuff
When they see you coming, niggas take off running
From you it's true, oh yes they do
One day he gon' say you crowding my space
One day he gon' say you crowding my space
I said one day he gon' say you crowding my space
One day he gon' say you crowding my space so, pack
light
Pack light, mm, pack light, pack light, ooh ooh
Girl I know, sometimes it's hard and we can't let go
Oh when someone hurts you oh so bad inside
You can't deny it you can't stop crying
So oh, oh, oh, if you start breathin' babe
You won't believe it, it feels so much better, so much
better baby
Bag lady, let it go let it go let it go let it go oh
Girl you don't need it
Bet ya love could make it better
Bet ya love can make it better
Bet ya love can make it better, need someone to love
you right

JAI HUDSON

PART II

THE HEALING PROCESS

"You are strong enough to overcome all the difficulties, both physical and emotional all you need to do is to clearly understand situation, decide that you want to be happy again, and show to everyone that you actually have the strength to heal."

-By Mackolizac

JAI HUDSON

XI
TALK THE TALK

"MAN IN THE MIRROR"

Song by Michael Jackson

I'm gonna make a change
For once in my life
It's gonna feel real good
Gonna make a difference
Gonna make it right
As I turn up the collar on
My favorite winter coat
This wind is blowing my mind
I see the kids in the street without enough to eat
Who am I to be blind?
Pretending not to see their needs
A summer disregard, a broken bottle top
And a one man soul
They follow each other on the wind ya know
Cause they've got nowhere to go
That's why I want you to know
I'm starting with the man in the mirror
I asking to change his ways
And no message coulda been any clearer
If you wanna make the world a better place
Take a look at yourself, and then make a change

JAI HUDSON

I GOT YOU

Women have been strong since creation. We bear children, we raise strong men, we have demanding careers, we have everything needed to nurture another living being, and we keep the world going. Most women don't even know how much power they have. They have allowed "dark forces" to diminish their power. With all the strength women possess, we have to protect our children. No more fears of being abandoned by a man, or fearful of change. We as women have to reach that point of wanting change and wanting to be happy so badly that it outweighs the fear. We have a responsibility to save our children. Period.

We have to remember we are not our circumstances. And we do not have to be a product of our environment. We can break the cycle and the silence. There are certain traits we take on, passed along from our

parents, and they received traits from their
parents, and so on. We learn our belief
system and how to survive from our parents.
Have you ever realized every family has an
overall theme or dysfunction they are trying
to overcome? It's usually something
experienced throughout generations. Just
like there are diseases that are hereditary,
there are dysfunctions that are as well.
Dysfunctions such as sexual abuse or
keeping secrets, not dealing with issues,
domestic abuse, alcohol abuse, and even
something as simple as how men treat
women and what women allow from their
mates, are passed on from generation to the
next. If a woman experienced domestic
abuse or alcohol addiction, It's almost
guaranteed that there are some traits of
abuse in the family history. And the
probability is very high for her child to suffer
from that dysfunction or surrounding effects

as well. I am not saying every case and family is the same. For some this may not be the case. But if it's not something as serious as abuse and addictions, it could be as simple as denial. Another thing I've noticed is that certain generations break the cycle. If our grandparents and parents couldn't, then we can. Each generation opens the door a little further to addressing the sexual abuse cycle.

We have to develop stronger bonds with our children — for they are truly the future. That's what kids want, they want to be heard, valued, loved, protected. Children are blessings and when a woman and man bring a child into the world, we have to recognize the gift. All children are God's gift and magical creation to the universe. We have to provide a loving and comfortable atmosphere so that children feel they can express themselves freely. Children also need to feel safe in knowing they will be heard and protected. That's how we stop the secrets. That's how we save our children, through acceptance and freedom of expression.

My mother didn't know what to do. From the outside looking in, anyone can judge and say what she could have done. But because she was taught to keep secrets and not deal with stuff at all, she didn't have the tools to know how to break the cycle. She was abused as well. This is in no way justification; it's just the facts and the cards my mother was dealt. For many women, it's tough to get out of a relationship when the person has manipulated you, controlled you, and abused you. Not to mention having a child, being married, and receiving a financial contribution from the man.

We have to support each other. Show our sisters that they can depend on us if they need to. Provide a shoulder or ear for women who may need someone to talk to in order to save their children. We have to recognize our power. Why do you think women were oppressed for so long — and still are to a certain extent? Fear creates control. Dark forces fear the true power of a woman. We cannot change others or the situation; sometimes, however, we can save our children and help our fellow women save theirs. We all need help one time or another, or a little motivation to leave, or just an ear to listen. These things cost nothing, just compassion, love, and care for another human being.

If a child confides in you, how you react is very important. The child needs to know that they are safe and loved. Embrace the child show them that telling was the correct thing to do.

JAI HUDSON

I know there are a lot of fears that come to mind when you are faced with something like this. A common worry for the woman is how she will get through it alone if her husband or partner is the perpetrator. If the abuser is of power or has authority, her fear might be disbelief from others. Mothers also fear their kids will be taken away. These are valid concerns, however, they are also fears and worry. Fear is merely designed to control and keep you away from love and saving the children who are our future. As long as you let fear and worry control you, the recurring cycle will continue. Let's break the cycles — stare fear in the face and break the imaginary control that fear has created. Together we can change the world!

Was it fear? Fear of not having a man? Fear of him hurting her? I had to come to the conclusion that my mother was a *woman* at the end of the day. He manipulated and hurt her tremendously. She feared being alone to raise two children. She feared not receiving love. She had the same fears all women have. I was so caught up in the fact that she was my mom, and mothers are supposed to protect their children. However, she was a woman in a dysfunctional relationship that made some poor choices.

My mom never used her abuse as a crutch and that's what I saw and learned. In turn, I kept it all in and just continued on with life. That is the typical response to abuse. There are so many people who have experienced abuse and are perceived as doing just fine. But they're not fine at all. I wasn't fine. Abuse caused a scar that was deep within and as much as I tried to cover it and hide it from others, the only solution was to heal it.

I know that it killed my mother slowly, knowing what country was doing to me. I know it killed her even more not knowing how to stop it and still be OK. I know that because I know my mother held a lot in. I knew my mom deep inside. I know it hurt her that I felt she didn't protect me. I never saw so many similarities with my mom until now. She was sexually abused by two men from her immediate family. No one seemed to know of her abuse except for the abusers. We differed because I had an outlet. She obviously felt she couldn't tell anyone. That was a lot for my mother to deal with and hold in as a child, and even as a woman. I can only imagine the guilt she felt on top of her own pain.

"The people who hurt you sleep fine at night....When are you? When is it your turn?" —Aleesha from Tell Someone Movement

JAI HUDSON

"DIARY"

Song by Alicia Keys

Lay your head on my pillow
And you can be yourself
No one has to know what you are feeling
No one but me and you
I wont tell your secrets
Your secrets are safe with me
I will keep your secrets
Just think of me as the pages in your diary
I feel such a connection
Even when you're far away
If there's anything that you fear
Call 4894608 and ill be there

JAI HUDSON

XII

FORGIVENESS

"BIG GIRLS DON'T CRY"

Song by Fergie

I need some shelter of my own protection, baby
To be with myself and center
Clarity, peace, serenity
I hope you know, I hope you know
That this has nothing to do with you
It's personal, myself and I
We've got some straightenin' out to do
And I'm gonna miss you like a child misses their
blanket
But I've got to get a move on with my life
It's time to be a big girl now
And big girls don't cry
Don't cry Don't cry Don't cry
The path that I'm walking
I must go alone
I must take the baby steps till I'm full grown, full grown
Fairy tales don't always have a happy ending, do
they?
And I foresee the dark ahead if I stay
I need to be with myself and center
But it's time for me to go homeIt's getting late and
dark outside
Clarity, peace, serenity

FIRST STEP

I learned to forgive on March 20th, 2014. I never thought that day would be the last conversation I had with my mom. Let me back up for a moment and explain how I got to this day.

So that major recurrence of the past had resurfaced for the last time. The day before it did, I watched "Iyanla Fix My Life" on Oprah Winfrey's *OWN* network, and learned about intention. They spoke about *identifying your intention* when in certain situations. For instance, when you are about to have an uncomfortable conversation, if you identify your intention for the conversation it makes it less uncomfortable for you. That made sense because the biggest thing about uncomfortable discussions for me was fear of something – maybe a fear of confrontation or fear of truth, or expectations. When you

JAI HUDSON

determine what your intentions are, it makes it easier and you are clear on what you want to accomplish. So there are no disappointments. You can't control another person's reaction to something but you can have control over knowing what the purpose is for you. Truly deciding what you want from a situation. *I also learned that women are women first:* even if they have children, they're still a woman first, and a mother second. That really changed my perspective on things. Those statements set off a light bulb within me.

I could finally see my mom clearly, without all the expectations the world, family, and I placed on her. I wanted her to protect, love, and save me. But now that I could strip all my wants away I could see her as simply a woman, flaws and all. I couldn't blame her anymore for my abuse, or not doing anything to stop it. I tried to step out of the situation and look at it from a different viewpoint.

I've always heard the saying "You change your reality when you change your perception." I had been holding on to this baggage ever since I was six years old. I suffered from resentment big time. And that is such a heavy emotion to carry all these years. It was time to let the load down. She was a woman first. And I knew what that felt like. I know what it feels like to be in a relationship and put the other person before self. I knew what it felt like to be in a relationship with someone who has a past they're not proud of. I could relate to loving someone and forgiving them for their past. So I could finally see my mother from another perspective — a perspective other than anger and hurt. None of this took away from what I experienced as a child, but I could finally see my mother from as her own person.

My life coach Misa Hylton also coached me. Yes, Misa the fashion stylist was now training to become a certified life coach. I woke up that fateful morning feeling like I need to get what I was feeling out. That I couldn't heal properly and move on without addressing the pain I had in my heart. I needed to express what I held in for so long to my mother. I wanted to have the conversation with my mom that I had tried to say for so long. I wanted to address what happened so we could both be free. I decided I would write her via text, so that I could release all I needed to without interruptions.

Previously, when I addressed the situation, I could never express myself completely because I saw it made my mom uncomfortable. She knew me so well and she knew that by responding with discomfort, she could get me to retreat and not deal with it. I backed down because I never wanted to hurt my mom. But I was continuously hurt in the process. My intention this day was to express how her choices regarding my abuse made me feel. I never told my mother how her choices made me feel. Now that I could see qualities of my mother in me, and because we were both women, I could finally address what I felt. I could forgive her, and start to truly heal.

So as I sat on the Metro North train, travelling from Harlem to Westchester, I decided to do it. I had taken this ride several times but this day felt different. In the past, I had always confronted my mother face-to-face. It never resulted how I needed it to. So I decided to text her all of my feelings.

Even though I texted her, I could feel her vulnerability through text. She had major

JAI HUDSON

regrets with how she dealt with my abuse. I could feel it. Everything felt different. When I addressed it this time my intention was to express myself and truly let her know how I felt. When she told me she was sorry and really wanted us to be close again and that she missed us, that satisfied my soul and I could finally let go of the pain.

I responded, "I forgive you."

RELEASING THE PAST AND EMBRACING FORGIVENESS

Forgiveness is not something that you do for the other person. Forgiveness is something that you do for you. Until I was able to forgive, I carried around hurt, anger, hate, resentment, sorrow, and many other painful feelings. These are all deep emotions that affected my body, the way I saw myself, the way I saw other people, and the way I viewed the world. Not forgiving kept me stuck in all of these negative emotions. It was like invisible shackles on my ankles and wrists. Actually, you can add a shackle around my neck too. I had to release myself of these restrictions because I was the only one with the key. The key was forgiveness.

On March 20th, God pushed me to address what was done to me, with the intention of getting all that I held in for so long out. I looked forward to a new relationship with her. The future was looking bright. A weight was lifted from my heart.

I didn't know it would be my last time telling her what I was dealing with inside. The last time I would tell her physically that I loved her so much. The last time we would ever talk again. No more learning about her childhood, no more updates on family, no more hugs from my mom. That day I learned the true meaning of forgiveness.

JAI HUDSON

"FREEDOM" THEME SONG FROM PANTHER MOVIE

Song by Various Artists

(Freedom) Turn us loose, set us free from all the
chains that bind me
(Freedom) Let us run in our own direction
(Freedom) Let us go, set us free from all this
propaganda and lies
That your people try to teach us
I know why you would like to bring us down
Because we have all the dirt on you
You try to tell us that our lives don't mean a damn
But we know so much better so we're gonna take our
freedom
(Freedom) Freedom for my body (Freedom, freedom)
Freedom for my mind (Freedom) {Oh, no, oh, no, no}
(Freedom) Freedom for my body
(Freedom) Freedom for my mind [Freedom] (Freedom
for my spirit, yeah)
All this time you've been tellin' us these lies
But now we've finally figured out your game
You thought that we would never wise up
But we showed you how a black female can do her
thing

(Left Eye)
Whoever said these are the things that you can do
And the things you ain't supposed to?
So am I further when I think I'm getting closer?

JAI HUDSON

That's when I tend to think of RosaHow Rosa took a
seat to make a stand
But now, in standing, we've gotten more
demandingThey never thought in planningThat a wish
for us to sit would be a dose of this fucking
rollercoaster
Whether tradition or religion, why you question my
decision?
Why you spend up all your time trying to get into my
mind?
How everybody and their mama
Gots to add to all my drama, mad drama
Hell if I'm gonna keep my dominating, feministicHell-
creating CrazySexyCool, Black assIn the palms of
your player-hater's stance
My only chance of being free is to fly within me
And it's illegal to kill a fuckin' eagle
A bird is never more important than my people
I guess we didn't need him so I took away his
freedom

(MC Lyte)
My spiritual awareness leads me to believe
That you're doubting the sisters to come with the
peace
We've been together since Jah created water
The African border, celebration is in order
Pop the cork and give champagne to the storkThat
brought the Lyte to my Mama in New York
African I come again + again
You kick me down, I get back up
I'm comin back in multiples of 10

JAI HUDSON

XIII

BREAKING THE CYCLE

"BE FREE"

Song by Faith Evans
Original song by J. Cole

When I'm in denial
And it don't take no x-ray
To see right thru
My smile I know
I be on the go
And there ain't no drink out there that can numb my
soul
No, no, no, no
All I wanna do is take the chains off
All I wanna do is break the chains off
All I wanna do is be free
All I wanna do is be free
All I wanna do is take the chains off
All I wanna do is break the chains off
All I wanna do is be free
Tell me why
Every time I step outside
I see my people die ohhh
I letting you that it ain't no gun that can kill my soul
No, no, no, no, no
All I wanna do is take the chains off
All I wanna do is break the chains off
All I wanna do is be free
All I wanna do is take the chains off
All I wanna do is break the chains off
All I wanna do is be free

JAI HUDSON

I DISLIKE MONDAYS

March 24th, I woke up feeling pretty much how I always felt. Nights have always been tough for me. Not to mention I hated Mondays. Everyone seems to be so serious on Mondays. That used to really irk me. *Does being stiff and serious really mean things are getting done?* No not really, but that's how some people treat Monday mornings. While I was in the shower I missed a call from my sister. So I read the text from her saying, "Mommy passed out, she's in the hospital." I immediately thought to myself, *was this like before*? My mom had a stroke in 2010 because of diabetes. Was this situation the same as before? I called my sister to find out what was happening. She said Teresita (her co-worker) called her and told her that my mother passed out. Something told me this wasn't like before.

JAI HUDSON

I rushed to the hospital and when I got there I saw that it was different. She took an access-a-ride to work that morning as usual. When she arrived to the 8th floor she walked over to clock in. Teresita said she saw my mother come in from down the hall and called out her name. "Donna..." But my mom did not reply. Teresita said she looked at her in a *dazed and confused* way. Then suddenly my mom dropped to the floor. She went into cardiac arrest. Teresita screamed out and ran over to her, She frantically tried to wake her. As others gathered, two male co-workers rushed to her side, applying CPR. After 40 minutes, EMT from the hospital across the street relieved the co-workers applying CPR. They were able to get a heartbeat but she never came to and was without oxygen for 40 minutes. They rushed her across the street to NY Presbyterian Hospital. My mom was having seizures every five minutes. So they put her in a coma, cooled her body temperature down, and there was still no progress. I watched that monitor everyday, all day. From the time I came into the hospital room till when I left. Before they did tests and after. When my stepfather was there and when he wasn't. I felt like that was my only way to listen to her heart and feel what she was feeling.

I couldn't believe this was happening. I had just forgiven her and we were about to have this new relationship. I was excited about that. I stayed by her side. Talking to her, playing music —Luther Vandross, "Amazing Love" — our favorite song, rubbing her hands and feet, anything I could do to keep her with me. To let her know I was there. Even though I wasn't physically around her like my sister in recent years, I felt so close to her at that moment.

JAI HUDSON

Remembering all the days when it was just the two of us. I knew my mother's true spirit. I knew my mom's true heart. I spoke to her, I lay with her, I washed her face, and I kissed her on her forehead. I didn't want her to ever feel I was giving up.

TAKING THE POWER BACK

On March 24th I forgave my mother's husband, my abuser, country. I had to let go of all the anger inside that was holding me back. I sat in my Misa's car for a moment. I needed a break. Suddenly, something just came over me. I couldn't believe the possibility that I was losing my mother. I cried hysterically. One of those cries when you can in no way control how you sound or look. I needed to get that out. I'm so glad I was able to do that and that I had someone like Misa there as a shoulder to lean on. She then said something to me that really

JAI HUDSON

affected me. She said that I needed to forgive him too, so that my mom and I could be free. Maybe my mom was waiting for that. Waiting for me to forgive him. Although, I didn't want her to go anywhere, I also didn't want her holding on for something like that. I'd rather her hold on for her own life. We had reached new heights in our relationship just four days ago.

However, at that time I didn't know how I could even get to that place where I could forgive him and it would be genuine. It seemed like the biggest mountain in front of me. I couldn't stand to be in the same vicinity as him. If I was going to forgive him, I had to go all the way. All I could do was pray for the strength and for God to lead me over that mountain.

I walked into the hospital room. My sister and her father were standing on opposite sides of the bed. I paused for a moment. A sudden strength and power took over. A courage that seemed familiar but I couldn't describe it if I tried my hardest. I was going to do it now. It was like my body took over because I walked straight over to him and said… "I forgive you." I then hugged him. He responded, "I love you Jacquetta." *I know what you're thinking.* That's big! I know, it was big to me too. I don't know who I was at that moment. I know it happened because my sister witnessed it, but it felt like a dream. It was as if something jumped in my body and completed the task. I didn't know how I was going to do it but somewhere deep inside I really did.

In the beginning, my mom's eyes were open and she still had the ability to squeeze my hands. The first two days she was having seizures, so she'd open her eyes looking into space as if she was experiencing the pain of a seizure. *It felt like she wanted to say something.* But of course, the doctors said she wasn't coherent and that was just an effect of the seizures. A day later her eyes were closed, and she wasn't able to swallow and breathe at the same time. Each day she became more and more lifeless. I never saw her eyes again. However, I still felt her spirit. Even when her best friends Debra and Ronnie came from North Carolina, we reminisced and conversed as if my mom was her regular self. We laughed and we recited her favorite sayings to her. My mom had some phrases that she was known to say all the time. One of them was "Tired ass." Another was calling her close friends and family "Baby," pronounced "bay bay." I wish you could hear her voice; she said those phrases a special way, the Donna way. I'd give anything to hear her call me a "tired ass" or "bay bay" again. I know everyone who knew my mother wishes the same. But I felt she was still there with me. During this time I leaned heavily on my new family. Misa, Mimi, Misa's mom, Kim Snow, and Wouri all came to the hospital to be there for me.

My sister went home to be with my nephew Nathaniel "Boo-boo," her son. My sister had a son the previous year and my mother stayed at my sister's house helping her care for Boo-boo. Funny thing, my nephew looks just like my mom. My sister resembles her father, so it's a beautiful feeling to see my mom every time I look at my nephew.

So after everyone left it was just Mom and me. Similar to how my life began. We spent two long days together. I told her how much I loved her. I told her if she stayed I would change my life to take care of her. I told her I needed her. I slept holding her hand the entire time. I didn't want to let it go.

JAI HUDSON

She never let mine go, so I didn't want to release hers. I wanted her to know I would always be there and that she could always count on that. It was such a blessing that I got to spend that time with my mom alone. Finally what I wanted. I wish it wasn't under these circumstances, but this being God's plan, I was thankful for the time. Period.

WHEN WE REMINISCE OVER YOU

I thought about this one time when I was young. My mom bought me a herringbone chain with my name highlighted in diamond cuts. Because my name had nine letters and was on a herringbone, it was super noticeable. I love my herringbone chain.

One day, actually the first time I wore the chain, we were on the C train going to Albee square mall downtown Brooklyn. As the train passed Kingston Avenue, a boy walked over and stood near the doors in front of where

JAI HUDSON

we were sitting. Weird thing is I looked at him and he kept looking away, but at the time I didn't think anything of it. When we reached Nostrand Avenue the doors opened and then the conductor called out to prepare for the closing doors. Suddenly, the boy lunged towards me, grabbing my chain. He ripped it off my neck and slid through the doors as they closed. It all happened so fast. I couldn't believe what just happened. I looked at my mother in disbelief. I stood up and she grabbed my hand. I sat back down next to her and she held my hand tight as we continued on with our trip. I looked at the faces of the people on the train in disbelief. I received my first lesson of BedStuy: do or die or get robbed. My mother and I never spoke of it again.

I also thought about a time my mom and I were going to King's plaza on the B46 bus. I had to be around 3 or 4 years old. I loved

JAI HUDSON

going to King's Plaza to shop for sneakers,
but mainly because they had Mrs. Fields
cookies. As soon as I walked through the
mall doors I smelled the scent of chocolate
chip cookies. Yum, I loved Mrs. Fields
cookies. As we pulled up to the shopping
mall, my mom grabbed my hand and we
exited through the rear doors of the bus.

Suddenly, this lady that I had seen on the
bus came over to us. I loved to people
watch. However, most people didn't even
know I was observing. As I watched this
lady, I saw that something was different
about her. She was different. Because I was
so young, I usually grouped certain people in
categories based on speech, movements,
eye contact, etc. That's how I learned. So I
basically put this lady in the category
consisting of this weird lady downstairs from
me on the 4th floor and this little boy who
people said had digested lead paint so he

was a little different. The lady on the bus
gave off a feeling that was familiar, like these
two people I had known.

Suddenly, the lady grabbed my other
hand and tried to pull me away from my
mother. It was like a tug of war game. What
was this lady trying to do? Was she trying to
take me away? Forever? It was now
apparent she was mentally challenged or
something. I didn't understand this at three
years old. My mom picked me up with so
much strength I felt the lady's hand release
mine with force. I buried my face in my
mother's neck as she carried me away
quickly. All I could hear was my mom cursing
the lady out. Everything happened so fast. I
couldn't believe what just happened.

I started to think kidnapping and taking
children or even taking things from children
was normal. It was happening all around me
and most importantly it was happening to

JAI HUDSON

me. I don't remember the rest of King's
Plaza that day. After that day, Mrs. Fields
wasn't so yummy anymore. And of course,
we never spoke of it again.

I never bought up uncomfortable
situations with my mom. It was just too
painful. I wasn't sure what the reaction would
be. So I just left it alone. I thought about all
the times we shared. I thought about all the
things I loved about her. Her smile, her high-
pitched voice, how she boasted about me at
her job every time I came to see her. When
I'd hug her I felt at home, felt like she
supported me and believed in me. I thought
about that hard exterior she displayed to the
world but was the most loving and sensitive
person I knew. I thought about how even
though she didn't know what I really did as a
career, she always believed in me. That was
empowering in itself. I thought about the fact
that she loved me so much. I thought about

the genuine care in her eyes. I thought about the fact that I could be losing the person who bought me into this world, my guardian angel on earth. All these things we might not ever get the chance to talk about again. Well, not physically anyway.

Those two days were truly special. I'm so grateful I was able to share those moments with her. I observed and took pictures on my phone of the numbers on the machine. The numbers that monitored her heart and breathing started out in the 80s, 90s, etc. So after those last two days we shared, and country came back, I couldn't understand why her numbers were dropping so low. They were now 20, 19, and 18. I felt like she started to leave slowly. The doctors saw no hope for my mom; they said she had little to no brain activity. They wanted to pull the plug. They explained that her quality of life would be poor. She would be totally

JAI HUDSON

dependent. I couldn't even start to picture that in my mind, but I was ready for whatever was to come. The doctor told me, my sister, and country to think about what we wanted to do. I walked out of the doctor's private office, feeling like I couldn't believe this was happening. I was not going to give up on her. I overheard country telling someone on the phone that she was gone. I couldn't believe what I was hearing. She never gave up on him but he was pronouncing her dead already. I forgave him but I really disliked him and I know he was one of the reasons my mom was in this predicament. My mom was broken from the beginning. He abused her child, impregnated another woman, and mistreated her for a long time. I am not accusing him of anything I'm just saying he added to her pain.

On March 31st I went into my mother's hospital room to tell her that I had to go to

LA to work on a Keyshia Cole video. I received the news a few days ago. I debated taking the job, but something told me to do it. I just needed to see my mom before I left. When I walked in, I saw she didn't look the same as she did before I left. The day I went home to change clothes and rest, country stayed at the hospital. I didn't want to think he was doing something to her to deteriorate her life, but those thoughts definitely popped into my mind. Actually, to be perfectly honest, I thought about that quite a lot. However, if someone is negative, they're negative — call a spade a spade. "The first time someone shows you who they are, believe them." – Maya Angelou.

When I walked in, I could immediately feel that life had left her body and the hospital room. I stood at the doorway and looked at my mom. She looked very different from two days ago. She was sitting upward with one of her legs crossed Indian style. I felt so numb. I could see from where I was standing that her complexion was the palest it's been. I walked closer to her and saw that her tongue was lodged outside her mouth. The heart monitor that previously had a faster beeping sound had now slowed its tempo. Her breathing numbers and heart rate had decreased from the 80% range to 6, 7, and 8%. I walked close and touched her hand. Her hand was extremely swollen like an inflated balloon. I was losing her. I was losing my mom. I knew she was leaving me. I could feel it. I first thought maybe there was something I could do to bring her back, but when I walked into the room I felt that she had already transcended. And there was nothing I could do. She was ready to go.... I couldn't watch her go but I had to let her go.

I couldn't stay in that room and see my mom leave me, the only person who truly knew me. I loved her so much and there was so much I wanted to tell her. I wanted to show her the person I had become. Even with all that I have been through, I still believed. I was a new person and I thought I would get the opportunity to show the *new me* to my mom.

I kissed my mom on the forehead and held my lips against her head as I whispered- "I love you forever." I kissed her hand as a salute to her, for being an amazing woman and the best mother she knew how. I turned off her Luther Vandross playlist that we played repeatedly near her ears. I walked out of the room and headed straight to the elevators. I cried hysterically on the elevator and even as I walked to the car. I didn't know how I should feel. I just lost my mother and although I felt numb at that moment, it was such a monumental event in my life.

JAI HUDSON

I left for LA on the April 1st. When we arrived it was straight to work for us. Misa Hylton and I styled the Keyshia Cole "Rick James" and "Next Time" videos. I remember working on set trying my hardest to not break down. I spoke to Kim Snow while on set; she'd lost her mom a few years before. She sent me an excerpt from "Knocking on Heavens Door" by Katy Butler: "Acceptance starts with opening your heart to the reality that someone you love is approaching the end of his or her life. It is time to find ways to say, '*I love you. Please forgive me. I forgive you*'. That way, when the time comes to say goodbye you're ready for that too. You may not be able to fix your parents' suffering or make them whole, but you can heal your relationship."

I needed to read that. I was feeling a little guilty for coming to Los Angeles to do this video, but for some reason that was confirmation that I was where I should be. I received the opportunity to tell my mom I forgive her. That's a priceless gift.

The next day before we left the hotel for day 2 of the video shoot, I received a message from my sister saying they were told to come to the hospital immediately. My mom passed away on April 2, 2014. I dropped to my knees and spoke these words into the air as if I was standing over her hospital bed.

I just realized I've been searching for someone to be all you have been to me. All you showed me. How much you loved me. Unconditionally, I knew how important you were, I allowed the pain to keep division in my heart. You made me feel so safe. I didn't worry at all. Do you know how it feels to have that one person who will always have your back and lets you know everything will be OK? I love you so much mom. I know you are free. I know you can finally be happy. Thank you for being an amazing mom. My mom. I love you forever.

My mom made a lot of mistakes, but one thing I do know for sure is that she really loved (loves) me unconditionally. I always felt guilty about leaving my mother and sister in Queens. We had to learn a new way to be after all the abuse happened. My mother's job, our favorite restaurants, places away from country became our new way to be mother and daughter. The only places we could be alone. I always felt weird when we departed. She had to return back to the "dark place" and I returned back to my life.

I saw the real Donna Elcock. She presented the world with this happy and always smiling person. Which is a beautiful representation. But deep inside, she was pretending to everyone. There was a deep pain that never truly healed. I knew the real

Donna. She couldn't pretend with me. Now I accept the fact that God took me away and showed me a better life. That was my mother's choice as far as staying with country. So she had to go through it. Play the hand that she was dealt. However, that didn't have to be my destiny. So there was a blessing in disguise. That distance and me exploring the world was protection…that distance was *Grace.*

"ANGEL OF MINE"

Song by MONICA

I look at you, lookin' at me
Now I know why they say
the best things are free
I'm gonna love you boy you are so fine
Angel of Mine
How you changed my world
you'll never know
I'm different now, you helped me grow
You came into my life sent from above
When I lost all hope you showed me love
I'm checkin' for ya boy you're right on time
Angel of Mine
Nothing means more to me
than what we share
No one in this whole world can ever compare
What you mean to me you'll never know
Deep inside I need to show
You came into my life sent from above (Sent from
above)
When I lost all hope, you showed me love
I'm checkin' for ya, you're right on time (Right on
Time)
Angel of Mine (Angel of mine)
I never knew I could feel each moment
As if it were new,
How you changed my

JAI HUDSON

world you'll never know
I'm different now, you helped me grow
I look at you lookin' at me
Now I know why they say
the best things are free
I'm checkin' for ya, boy you're right on time

JAI HUDSON

XIV

HEAVEN COULDN'T WAIT

"I AIN'T MAD AT CHA"

Song BY Tupac

Rewind us back, to a time
was much too young to know
And even though we separated,
you said that you'd wait
I kiss my Mama goodbye,
and wipe the tears from her lonely eyes
Said I'll return but I gotta fight the fates arrived
Don't shed a tear, cause Mama I ain't happy here
I'm through trial, no more smiles, for a couple years
Unconditional Love (no doubt)
Talking bout the stuff that don't wear off
It don't fade
It'll last for all these crazy days
These crazy nights
Whether you wrong or you right
I'm a still love you
Still feel you
Still there for you
No matter what (hehe)
You will always be in my heart

JAI HUDSON

MOTHER DAUGHTER RELATIONSHIP

My relationship with my mom was different than any other relationship I've ever had. It was like we had a string attached to our hearts. I knew her heart and she knew mine. She listened to me. Our relationship was so special. I didn't have to say anything. She knew exactly how I felt. I guess that's because she carried me for nine months. That was the same for me. She didn't have to say anything I could tell by her eyes and energy. We were connected. We lost that connection when her husband began the abuse. It was hard to communicate the way we did before.

   She knew I had a good heart. She knew that I felt things deeply. She knew that I wanted to make her proud. I cared for my mom even with all the circumstances. I was angry yes, however, if she ever needed me I

JAI HUDSON

was there in the blink of an eye. I knew that was the same for my mom. She cared and loved me deeply.

YOU CAN GO HOME

After my mom passed on April 2, 2014, I began the process of healing. That was a very tough time for me I was searching for answers and comfort. Three months after she passed, I started attending Shaman sessions. Shaman healers are spirit healers and have a gift of communication with spirits and Angels. I was receiving coaching as well. Everyone can benefit from life coaching — doctors, top executives, pastors, police officers, teachers — everyone. A Shaman healer is like a life-coach that has a strong spiritual connection with angels and the spirit within. It's a gift of clairvoyance or the ability to connect with energies. My intention was to heal and hopefully be closer to my mom.

JAI HUDSON

This may sound a little bizarre but I believe in angels and I could feel my mother watching over me.

Nicola (my Shaman coach) had a very gentle spirit. We connected in a way where it was like she could see my soul. She coached me over the phone and conducted Shaman healing in-studio. She cleaned my chakras, and helped me unlock self-love and discover the spirit I lost. She also provided a therapy that I needed in order to cope with my mom's passing. At one of my shaman sessions, Nicola told me that the Angels asked that I release my mom so that she could "be free and experience a higher consciousness." I didn't understand what that meant. Release her?

Nicola explained. My mom was in limbo, sort of like an "in-between" state, a "golden cocoon." She was staying around to be close to me. To release her was to simply tell her that it was OK to go. When I heard this I immediately felt a moment of gratitude that my mom was "putting me first." She was sticking around for me? As beautiful as that was, I also didn't want to prevent her from finally being free. I went home and thought about what I was going to do. So many questions filled my head. We finally were having the type of relationship I wanted for so long. I felt her watching over me so close. In this state of limbo she was experiencing a lot of how I felt. It was difficult but I was starting to grasp the fact that she was no longer physically here. She had spent her whole physical life putting a man first and not herself. I wanted her to be happy. I wanted her to be free.

So I knew what I needed to do. I went to my next Shaman healing and told Nicola I had made my decision. So I lay on the masseuse table and closed my eyes. I was instructed to take deep breaths, in through my nose out through my mouth. Then Nicola began her spiritual connection.

"HEAVEN COULDN'T WAIT"
Song by Beyoncé
I fought for you the hardest,
It made me the strongest
So tell me your secrets
I just can't stand to see you leaving
But heaven couldn't wait for you
So go on go home

I started to feel a hot sensation all over my body. It felt as if my mom was there. A tear fell from my eyes. What I was feeling was so surreal and spiritually awakening for me. Suddenly, Nicola said that my mom wanted to tell me that, "If I continued to cry she wasn't going anywhere." *Wow,* I thought to myself, *that sounds just like my mom.* We

both couldn't stand to see each other cry. So
I wiped my eyes and said, *"Mom I want you
to be free. Go home. It's OK. I want you to
be happy. I love you so much! You can go
home."*

After I said this, I could feel the energy
shift in the room. (I hesitated leaving this part
in the book because everyone has his or her
own beliefs. However, this was my
experience. So please be open.) She was
free. I could feel it. I felt that lump in my
throat go away. I felt free too.

Nicola told me that the Angels wanted to
give me a gift. Wow, a gift? "Yes a gift," she
said. The Angels gave me the gift of *Grace*.
At this time I didn't understand what *Grace*
truly was. I've heard it a few times before,
but what did it really mean? I told her I
needed her to explain what was the gift of
Grace. She then told me to remember a time
when I received a blessing and didn't have

to work for it. When a magical life jacket was thrown to me without knowing its origin. A time I received a love that was given without any of my doing.

That is what Grace is. So I thought long and hard. I then told Nicola the first memory of Grace that came to mind.

XV

GRACE

JAI HUDSON

"FREE"

Song by DESTINY'S CHILD

Ain't no feeling like being free
When your minds made up
And your hearts in the right place yeah
Ain't no feeling like being free
When you done all you could
But was misunderstood
It's all good all good
Ain't no feeling like being free
I'm like an eagle set free
Finally I'm looking out for me
Ain't no feeling like being free
When your minds made up
And your hearts in the right place yeah yeah yeah

JAI HUDSON

MAGICAL LIFE JACKET

Living with Talia, her mom Sonia, and sister Alisha was an outlet provided by God. It was like God picked me up out of the situation I was in and put me in this place where I could be loved. And gave me a choice, a possibility. They took me in and I could finally escape the abuse.

Do you truly understand what that was for me? An end to fears of sleeping, fears of showing my beauty, fears of people knowing my stepfather was fondling me at night, anxiety each night that it would happen again, and worries he would rape me. Leaving my household provided me with the ability to breathe and relax my mind, body and soul. That was protection…I couldn't understand it back then. But I knew I was in the right place, even with my mom giving me a hard time about being away from home.

JAI HUDSON

Back then I thought I was just running away from home, but in reality I can look back and see it was truly a blessing from GOD.

So this was a memory of *Grace*. I didn't have to work for the love. I was saved in more ways than anyone could imagine. I had a way out. And I received a love that I didn't have to do anything to receive or maintain. In the past, I felt like if I kept quiet, got good grades, and worked hard my mom would choose me. She would protect me and love me. However, Talia, Sonia, Alisha, and her family were the imaginary life jacket thrown out to me. God gave me grace and I didn't even realize it.

Then back when I was 21 years old, fresh from Los Angeles CA visiting with Talia, It was like I was chosen again for Grace. Not knowing my next steps in my journey I was blessed with Misa Hylton. She modeled what it was like for a strong Black woman in New York City *"making her mark"* in this entertainment business. I was in awe. She was taking risks in popular culture, creating headlines in fashion magazines, all while having 3 small children at home and in her late 20s. And yes she invited me into her world to learn and become the Jai I am today. It was like she put me under her nurturing wings and showed me the light. God used Misa. She may not know, but by including me in her wonderful family, she contributed to my beautiful and optimistic perception of hope. I still believe in beauty and I know that I could have all I dreamed of at night. It is possible. Misa showed me that all is attainable. I was witnessing her attain hers. Thank you!

So I told this to Nicola. These were times I felt I didn't have to work for love. It was a magical life jacket or invisible hand. That's what *Grace* is. When I think about all the situations I didn't have to work for love, protection, or a way out, that was Grace. When I really thought about it, I realized I have had a lot of *Grace*. So, to receive a gift of Grace from the Angels was a beautiful thing. Something I felt I needed at this time.

IT IS WHAT IT IS

It seems like when it rains it pours. Losing my mother was truly the toughest thing I have ever experienced. This was more emotionally painful than the abuse, it created a deeper emptiness than not having the love of my father, and was more physically impairing than overcoming the most difficult obstacle. This experience was always a hidden fear. I couldn't imagine my mom not being here physically. I can remember the look in my mother's eyes when I poked fun at her mom no longer being alive. Her tears back then expressed how I felt presently. I

JAI HUDSON

never prepared myself emotionally for something like this. Losing her meant, I was losing a major part of my heart. I was losing the other part of my childhood, the beautiful part, and the person who shared those memories with me.

I learned early on how to replace my emotions with other things, whether it be creativity, love, work, smoking, drinking, etc. It was just too much to feel. I always thought that if I let my emotions run free I might go mentally crazy. And I somehow started to attach feelings and emotions to being weak. Which is so far from the truth. Right before my mother's passing, I started to face my emotional disabilities head on. I stopped going around my pile of baggage and started to go through it, to deal with it. Do the work on me. I was tired of feeling disappointed and depressed. I wanted to love me more. Actually I wanted to love me the most.

JAI HUDSON

The world is in constant motion and time is quickly ticking. It's a moving cycle that felt to me like existing in a hamster wheel. It was spinning so fast and I was trying my hardest to stay afloat. I didn't deal with my needs because one, there wasn't enough time; two, there were bigger things to get through; and three, the past already happened anyway. But I had to stop and really think about what this meant. I was saying I didn't have time for me. This was someone else's perception of life because there was always time for me. This was my life. The world wouldn't happen (through my eyes) if I didn't happen. Once I gave up on me, there was no more world.

So I decided that I had all the time I needed to focus on myself. I started to realize that everyone connected to me was affected by my inability to love myself. It affected how I loved. It affected how I trust

others and God. I had to get off of the
hamster wheel and turn off the mental
clocks, and deal with me.

God has given each person the tools
needed to overcome the obstacles placed
before him or her. I had to think, *Would God
walk hand in hand through hardships and let
my hand go when it got too difficult?* I had to
think about when the most successful people
explain their road to success, it's usually
filled with many challenges, however, they
get through it and overcome. We all are
armed with whatever we need to conquer
our own personal trials and tribulations. So
it's not really about the success, it's more
about the lesson and the journey. That has
to be it, because I was still standing and my
life wasn't over yet.

It's more about learning lessons,
becoming wiser, or maybe just repeating
certain lessons until we actually get it and

grow. When I was able to truly grasp this concept, that's when I began to live and stop blaming others for my hardships. It was very difficult but I started to think about things differently. If nothing is coincidence and all things happen for a reason then there's a purpose for suffering and that purpose is to learn and grow. No pain is without purpose.

Writing these words was very therapeutic for me. My mother wanted me to write this book to help women and children heal from abuse. More times than not, the focus is placed on the abuser. The authorities investigate why the abuser abused and how we prevent it from happening again. What about healing the victim?

Through my experiences and telling my story, I healed. However, I didn't realize that's what was happening. I was healing through my experiences. Healing a past of pain and/or sexual abuse starts and ends with focus on self. I went to several therapy appointments, which were very helpful. However, I had to do the work. I had to stop playing the blame game, face my truth and take my power back.

Some may not have experienced sexual abuse but have some of the same holes and veils. I continually think about little six-year-old Jai, who felt alone and was hurt over and over. The feelings I developed about myself weren't caused solely by abuse. It was also how my abuse was dealt with emotionally and physically.

The past was preventing me from truly living. It's like imaginary chains restricting me from true happiness. It was all about the stories I told myself. It became my script. It's how I blamed myself. It was all my fault, all the things that were done and not done to me. It was my inner critic telling me those things. That's the voice that told me to give

JAI HUDSON

up and that I deserved the abuse. It was the shadow that was standing in front of me, hindering me from my true purpose.

However, I had to really pay attention to what was holding me back. I had fears of not being good enough. I felt that I wasn't worthy of what I dreamed of. I could go on and on. Do you recognize the common denominator? It was *me*. I was standing in my own way. I was stopping me — not my stepfather anymore, not my mother, not anyone else. *It was me.*

XVI

GOTTA FIND A PEACE
OF MIND

JAI HUDSON

"PEACE OF MIND"

Song By Lauryn Hill

I gotta find peace of mind
I know another cord...
I gotta find peace of mind
See, this what that voice in your head says
When you try to get peace of mind...
I gotta find peace of mind, I gotta find peace of mind
He says it's impossible, but I know it's possible
He says there's no me without him, please help me
forget about him
He takes all my energy, trapped in my memory
Constantly holding me, constantly holding me
I need to tell you all, all the pain he's caused, mmmm
I need to tell I'm, I'm undone because, mmmm
He says it's impossible, but I know it's possible
He says it's impossible without him, but I know it's
possible
To finally be in love, and know the real meaning of
A lasting relationship, not based on ownership
I trust every part of you, cause all that I... All that you
say you do
You love me despite myself, sometimes I fight myself
I just can't believe that you, would have anything to do
With someone so insecure, someone so immature
Oh you inspire me, to be the higher me
You made my desire pure, you made my desire pure
Just tell me what to say, I can't find the words to say
Please don't be mad with me, I have no identity
All that I've known is gone, all I was building on

JAI HUDSON

I don't wanna walk with you, how do I talk to you
Touch my mouth with your hands, touch my mouth
with your hands
Oh I wanna understand, the meaning of your
embrace
I know now I have to face, the temptations of my past
Please don't let me disgrace, where my devotion lays
Now that I know the truth, now that it's no excuse
Keeping me from your love, what was I thinking of?
Holding me from your love, what was I thinking of?
You are my peace of mind, that old me is left behind
You are my peace of mind, that old me is left behind
He says it's impossible, but I know it's possible
He says it's improbable, but I know it's tangible
He says it's not grabable, but I know it's have-able
Cuz anything's possible, oh anything is possible
Please come free my mind, please come meet my
mind
Can you see my mind, oh
Won't you come free my mind?
Oh I know it's possible

JAI HUDSON

GOT HOLES?

I began to realize the only way to feel better was to stop running from my past. I had to get to the core of my problems and give up some of the baggage I was carrying. There was so much emotional baggage I was still holding on to. I had to finally let the load down, one by one. The only way was to deal with it —address it head on and stop running away.

When a child experiences abuse or some form of lack in the love, security, protection or emotion, a hole forms. A hole is something that has not been addressed. Something you may battle with deep inside. A hole can be created by not having your father in your life, or even with an unhealthy overly protective parent. Situations like this result in our ability to adapt to whatever our circumstances are and to continue on with life. We adjust and usually find substitutions to cope. Most times the substitutions are temporary. The hole won't disappear because no matter how much you try to cover up a hole or fill it with substitutions, the hole needs to be healed. Drinking, denial, avoidance or even cigarettes only masks the scar: the hole is still there and still needs healing.

The holes that were created in me directly affected my sense of *self-worth*. I couldn't recognize my power at all. These childhood events were the seeds and that grew low confidence and low *self-love*.

I avoided "my holes." Whenever anything resurfaced that related to the past, I ran. However, things were starting to change and my running away wasn't having the same results. Now things were becoming more and more heavy and tougher to run from.

As life was unfolding, I was not aware of the hole created within. I began to believe that my voice didn't matter, and my self-love was non-existent, and I was emotionally disabled. I didn't feel good about me at all. I put everyone before I put myself, I loved hard and gave my all to so many, however didn't know the first thing about loving and caring for me. I usually filled my holes with external substitutions —sex, relationships, cigarettes, alcohol, work, marijuana, running away, isolation, etc. Because these are all substitutions, the cycle continued.

I became a yeller and very withdrawn. When a situation triggered my emotions, I yelled and projected my voice so that I could be heard. That's how I protected myself. That's how I figured I could get people to listen. How a person reacts to holes from childhood varies for everyone.

When I was a kid I used my imagination to escape the pain. When I became an adult, the way of the world is to put away childish things. So I stopped daydreaming and replaced it with people, materials, drugs, alcohol, behaviors, etc. However, the only "hole fillers" that are truly gratifying and permanent are *Self* and God (God means *Love*). I had to learn that. Whenever I was hurt by something, I masked the pain — sometimes with sex, or maybe it was a cigarette or a drink, or something as simple as shopping. I automatically filled my holes with external things and it started to feel like a never-ending cycle, and those holes never got filled.

Recurring issues constantly appeared in my relationships. I'd give my all to a person, wanting them do the same for me. And if I felt the person didn't, I'd slowly put them in the "hurt" category that was created by my mother's behavior. But there was deeper meaning to this, if I was willing to stop the blame game and take responsibility for how I was feeling. Internally, I was placing expectations on others. I wanted to be protected and cared for. And by not giving me their all, that meant — I interpreted it to mean — that *I didn't matter.* It reinforced my lack of self-worth, and my belief in myself. That's what was happening inside of me, one of my many recurring "hole" themes.

PRACTICE I

(Practice makes Perfect!)

JAI HUDSON

HOLE FILLERS

What holes do you have? What caused your holes? What do you fill your holes with? How can you start to fill your holes with self? Ask yourself these questions — questions we often advise others to ask themselves. The first step is identifying the issue troubling you. Whether it's low self-esteem, missing the love of your father, or feeling emotionally empty... identify what's missing and think about how YOU can fill you with only YOU. Once you determine what holes you have, you can now start to fill yourself up.

CLAIM IT!

Stop reading for a moment and think about how you want to feel inside. This is very important for manifesting what you want. It's easy to know what we don't want, but sometimes it takes more effort to know what we do want. Find the words to describe the feeling you want to have inside. Claim how you want to feel and be. State those qualities aloud. As an example, I'll state mine: I Want To Be Without Fear, I Want To Love Freely Without Restrictions With Healthy Boundaries, I Want To Let Go Of All The Doubts I Put On Myself, I Want To Live My Potential, and I Want To Be Happy!

Let YOUR words resonate in your soul. They are your personal guidelines for filling your holes. And you can add to the ultimate feeling you want to have any time you want. Once you claim how you want to feel, this becomes your navigation system for reaching your goals. If a situation or something that's still only a possibility doesn't match your desired feelings, then it's not right for YOU.

JAI HUDSON

GOALS

This was my goal for myself. It's easy for us to set goals regarding others, even for work, but when do we ever set goals for how we want to feel? Once I determined how I wanted to be and feel, I was able to look at each feeling and determine what was holding me back from having that feeling authentically. I wanted to be fearless so *why was I fearful* and what was I afraid of? I was older, and wiser, but still holding on to old ways.

I had to go back to those moments in time. When the holes were created. By getting to the core and truly doing the work needed I was able to heal the wound at its core. It was like clearing a hoarded house out internally, one room at a time — bag by bag. It was freeing because figuring me out left me feeling empowered. A lot of the things I was holding onto were protection for that 6-year-old little girl. Back then I was fighting hard to maintain. However, I am grown now and those protection mechanisms do not serve me any more.

When I cleared away the feelings that no longer served my life in the present moment, I was left with less resentment and blame. It was so freeing. It's also guaranteed that the outside will mirror the inside. The sooner I dealt with it, or in other words quit going around my holes and became more *whole,* the sooner I could reach a place of healing and happiness.

FILL YOU UP

Remember the shapes game as a child? It came in different forms but the one I had looked like a square plastic box. It had a different color on each side of the 3 dimensional box; red, blue, yellow, green, etc. It had a number of holes in different shapes on the box that taught a small child about shapes, among other lessons. The object of the game is to put the shaped piece into its correct hole. If the shape didn't match the hole, it wouldn't fit in. That's sort of like how it was attempting to fill my personal "holes" (i.e., low self-worth) with the incorrect "hole fillers." They never truly fit. I had to learn to fill the holes with self and love, because that's the truest fit. The only person who could fill my holes left from childhood is me.

When my mother passed away, that was the kick-start of my healing process. I started to deal with my baggage. Face myself. Face that shadow standing in front of me. Finally deal with me. Her passing forced me to hurry up the process — life wasn't waiting for me to get prepared. Sometimes it happens like that. The choice is yours; either deal with it, or be forced to deal with it through life experience.

Are you able to step out of your way and allow yourself the possibility? Will you allow yourself the opportunity to completely let go of whatever it is holding you back? Are you able to choose joy and a higher standard of self-love? Rewrite the stories and patterns of survival to reflect the now? Stare fear in the face and break the chains that have kept you captive? Can you start to let go of the past?

We have to forgive ourselves. What are you waiting for? Jump off that fast-spinning hamster wheel and make the commitment to yourself. Make a vow to unveil yourself from the forces that have tried to dim your light. Chose to go through your baggage and start to organize your life. Make the commitment to fill your holes with the true essence of you.

JAI HUDSON

PRACTICE II

JAI HUDSON

FILL ME UP SCOTTY

Everyone has holes. Life can be like a video game, navigating through the challenges and acquiring certain things along the way that can help or hinder our path. We gain certain experiences or tools to help us complete the challenge. There are different players to choose from that have specific strengths. Unlike a video game though, in life no matter how many tricks you learn, or weapons you acquire, what will bring you to victory is always YOU.

Filling our holes with self simply means that when you feel like you are missing something, instead of expecting the solution to come from another person, substance, or a fear-based action, fill you with you. When you feel that feeling of lack, gently inquire within to figure out where it comes from. Trace it back to its origin and then try to think of an emotion that solely comes from you to fill that hole. For example, let's say you have trust issues. Looking for its origin, you may remember abandonment by your father. Without your even being aware of it, that hole of abandonment was filled with fear, anger, inability to love and trust, or some other way of protecting that hole. As an adult, you may still find it challenging to trust people in your life; you're still protecting that hole, rather than healing it.

Now, let's look at an abandonment experience from a different perspective. Mentally review that time when your dad left. Accept that his absence was also a gift, as tough as that may be. Why was it a gift? Because you now have the chance to be who you really are. Forgive him. Now fill that hole of lack of trust with you. You can reframe how you perceive the event: that one situation does not define your entire life. Release expectations of others, because no one in your present is the father who left you and they can't fill that hole. Know that God, Source, the Universe is always working WITH you.

So, whenever you have that feeling of abandonment, instead of inviting someone over to distract you from it, or having a cigarette, or even isolating yourself so that you won't feel, stop and do something different. Listen to a song that makes you feel good, do your makeup if that is therapeutic; do whatever it is that makes you feel good. In this way, you interrupt negative mental habits and eliminate any possibility of blame or reactivity toward the other person, and address the issue at its core. In turn,

JAI HUDSON

there are no disappointments from others,
only a feeling of fullness from within — you
have the power!

JAI HUDSON

XVII

WISDOM

"CAN YOU HEAR ME?"

Song by Missy Elliott & TLC

I know you in real good hands
With God but damn I miss you
Aaliyah if you see Left Eye will you tell her
That me and Boz miss her too
Cause no ones gonna fill her space
TC L not replace
Yall the reasons we learned to love
Fly high with your 22 doves
One day we'll see her again
With the same old beautiful smile
Crazy but sexy cool
She'll be rapping them same old songs

Lisa can you hear me
We hope that you're proud of us
TLC has come along way
But it's never been the same
Since you had to go
Cause the healing process will
be long and slow
Aaliyah I know you in a safer place
You face to face with the creator
And our maker
And if you and Left-Eye
happen to chat tell her
Me and Tionne we know that she much safer
If you see Biggie Smalls up in the clouds tell him

JAI HUDSON

He's still the illest MC we had around
2pac there is only one
Big Pun RIP we say one
One day we'll see yall again
With the same old beautiful smiles
All styles so many styles
And y'all be doing the same old things
The last time we seen ya
We hope yall can change the world
Let them see how short life be
It would never be the same
since you had to go
To the music world yall are incredible

JAI HUDSON

EVERYTHING HAPPENS FOR A
GREATER REASON

I should be angry with my mother. I shouldn't be able to see all the great qualities within her. I should hate her and move on. But what does that anger and hate do? It shows up continuously over and over. All of the wanting my mother to protect me and to put me first kept showing up in different ways. I was angry she didn't do what "I would do." I was holding on to all these negative feelings. So who's really suffering at the end of it all? Suffering from the case of "*shoulda, woulda, coulda?*" She didn't do what I would have done. She isn't me. I needed to accept that truth, big time. She has her own life path, her own lessons to learn and overcome. Facing and accepting this reality is what really allowed me to let go and move on.

As a child going through abuse, I had my own truth about the situation. We all have

JAI HUDSON

our own truths. The abusers have theirs and my mother had hers also. *Everyone's truth matters.* No one perspective is right or wrong. Our perspective is usually the motivation and story behind each person's life path. Perspectives are also influenced and shaped by the truths of past generations. Beliefs in my family were passed along generation to generation. However, the story changes. With each generation there is a possibility of change and progression. There are also new factors involved.

For example, take the women in my family. My grandmother had her set of beliefs of keeping family secrets, which was passed along to my mother. That was the "code" of the family: "Keep family business, family business." Of course, I knew the code of the family and tried to keep secrets too, however there were new elements involved.

JAI HUDSON

I have a different set of truths because mine included going against the family code by speaking up to my mother regarding my abuse, confiding in my best friend, and also speaking up with this book. The generations before me were complacent with life, following the tribal paths of the family. My family consisted of accountants, finance, and stable city jobs. I was different I spoke up, I'm interested in the arts, and had dreams bigger than our 1865 Fulton Street apartment could contain.

So what I'm basically saying is that I learned *things can change.* There is hope. We do not have to be a product of our environment and circumstances. We no longer have to follow old tribal ways when they no longer serve. We can be different. My grandmother most likely didn't feel this way. If she did, my mother's circumstances would be different and mine would be also.

JAI HUDSON

My grandmother was on her own raising her children. I had Mama King's wisdom growing up and she had a strong influence on me as a child. She taught me to speak up.

According to a post called "A Few of the Many Ways We Distort Reality," published by Psychology Today by Karyn Hall PhD: "One of the choices you have when faced with a problem is to change your perception of the problem. People sometimes resist altering their perceptions, believing they are right in what they see, hear, and remember. The truth is that your perceptions are often inaccurate, particularly in emotionally charged situations. So one way of being more open to changing your perception is to consider the ways your perceptions maybe inaccurate."

I learned to step outside of my life and world, and look at the entire situation from a different view other than mine. This concept assisted with my understanding of why pain happens and what life is truly about. Instead of being so mad at the things I couldn't change. I started to focus on the one thing that I could change for sure, and that was me. I couldn't change the abuse. I couldn't change my mother and I couldn't make her leave him. It was what it was. But the key to change started with me looking at my challenges differently. I had the power to change how I felt, but it started with how I looked at situations.

LET'S TALK ABOUT IT

We have to start the conversation regarding sexual abuse and molestation. A major reason why it's so common is because sexual abuse is a taboo topic. It has become the subject we are just not comfortable talking about, but why? If we make it an everyday conversation, or when abusers are called out for their initial manipulations, maybe we can make the perpetrators start to feel uncomfortable. The tables can turn. They will start to feel like they can't manipulate children to keep secrets. Sexual abuse and molestation will not be a secret anymore.

It may seem impossible. But it's not, and we have to start somewhere. The communication and dialogue regarding sexual abuse must increase. It needs to become more a part of our everyday conversations. The abusers are hiding behind the fact that it's taboo and a disease. It's sort of like the abuse is understood because the perpetrator has a sickness. Authorities pacify the sickness with isolation, jail, and pedophile databases that expose abusers to the world. When we as adults become more comfortable with the topic of abuse, our children will as well. Besides, providing a comfortable environment of open communication builds trust, honesty, and confidence, children need to feel like they can express themselves. If not, they will grow to be adults unable to articulate who they are, with very low confidence in themselves and voice, and continuing the family code of keeping secrets. It' like a domino effect, passing the same tribal messages of hurt and pain generation to generation.

EXPLORE THE DARK

I hated that she let me go through it alone. I hated that my voice wasn't heard. I hate that she didn't protect me. I hate that she allowed him to hurt me over and over again. I hate that I felt she didn't love me. I hate that I felt she didn't love me enough. I hate that she seemed to love my sister more. I hated her — but now I feel so lost without her.

JAI HUDSON

I learned that it's OK to get it out by releasing all the emotions kept inside. I had to allow myself the freedom and acceptance of exploring my feelings. Some of my deep feelings were dark and I needed to get them out! I had been holding on to these strong feelings towards my mother ever since she made me choose whether country stayed or not. I was keeping all that inside. I had to release these negative emotions. Words can hurt, so imagine what it was doing to my body by keeping it all inside. After I acknowledged that I hated what my mother allowed me to go through, I felt free from that part of it. It was like those feelings had been weighing me down. The hatred was for something done in the past, and here I was in the present moment, still carrying this heavy weight from more than 10 years ago. I had to free myself if I truly wanted to experience freedom.

JAI HUDSON

YOU'RE IN CHARGE OF YOU

There's such a freedom in being in charge of you. Your mind, your body, your path, your beliefs… No one is to blame. Think about it, it's already a tough job just figuring yourself out. When we add someone else's life to the mission it becomes even more challenging. That's what happens when we blame someone. It's like having a casual conversation and when the topic of blame comes up, the go-to emotion is usually that feeling in the past where someone betrayed us and we blame him or her. Situations like this became a part of me — they became "my story or script." Not to diminish the abuse, but if I am in charge of me but blaming someone else for my emotional state, I am giving my power away to the person who betrayed me. So when I think about all the other emotions that drew up feelings from the past, I was powerless.

JAI HUDSON

Because I had given it all away. No wonder I felt drained, with many periods of low energy. I had to take my power back.

(Side Note: I chose to write country's name with a lowercase "c" as another way of owning my power. In college, when pledging for my sorority, whenever we wrote anything it had to be lowercase. We were not worthy of capital letters yet. It was like taking the power away from something. I chose to take the power that country had over me away, so that's why I chose to keep his name lowercase. This book is also not about country. country is just a symbol for so many challenges we are faced, whether it's sexual abuse, physical, alcoholism, etc.)

MY BELIEFS

We are all beams of light created to shine and give off a light that illuminates the universe. ***We are all individually, uniquely created: a one of a kind design.*** How beautiful is that? That's why we were created. That's what I believe. I believe we are all created with a purpose and from an idea. Meaning, we didn't just magically appear in our mother's stomachs. Nor was it as surface as just a sexual act. I believe there was a greater reason for our conception — a more special explanation for why we were created and gifted to our parents, families, and the world. I believe everyone has a purpose for their creation. With all good things there's also bad. With light, there's dark, if there's a down there's always an up. Life is about balance. So, since we are all wonderfully created, we will experience some form of opposition or challenges. Life is forever teaching us how to balance. That's my belief.

JAI HUDSON

VEILS

Abuse is like a veil. A veil means to cover or conceal. So a veil dims light temporarily. But when we simply remove the veil, our light can shine bright again. Deal with the "veils" and uncover them, and take your power back. It all starts with us. We have to get to the core of who we are. The *core* is the seed — the most important part of something. I believe I received challenges in order to learn and to overcome them. I started to realize that it was *my* emotions, *my* depression, and *my* recurring feelings. No one felt the exact emotions I felt. I had to take responsibility and accept that these were *my* lessons to learn — all mine.

I had to learn Forgiveness, Self Love, Self-Worthiness, Power in Voice, Fearlessness, Loving and accepting me, Trusting myself, Self-Happiness, Faith, Openness, Growth,

JAI HUDSON

Confidence, and Understanding the true meaning of Grace.

I had to get to the core and uncover the veils one by one. Forgiveness was the first step for me. All of the unhealthy emotions I was experiencing were dimming my light big time. Because I couldn't forgive in the past, anger, resentment, low self-love, etc. represented me in the present. They were my veils. These emotions disabled my heart. I couldn't be the light I was created to be because these heavy emotions I was holding on to darkened my light.

CHANGE VS FEAR

God doesn't give you more than you can handle. We are all armed with the wisdom and tools needed to overcome our individual struggles. Whatever the opposition may be, we are prepared. My mom and I could have stood together in unity to help put an end to

the stigma attached to sexual abuse.
However, we will now! My mom could have
protected me. She could have ended her
relationship with her husband and had faith
that a healthy love would find her again. She
could have done many things to change the
circumstances. However, that wasn't in the
cards. It wasn't part of her physical life
mission. But God stepped in. Spiritually, she
is my driving force for making a difference.
So with my loss, and her sacrifice, we will
change the world.

My mom stayed quiet about her abuse,
and she suffered. The woman who stays
with the pedophile is affected as well. Think
about all the depression, low self-esteem,
and psychological issues my mom faced. All
of her holes clouding her judgment and the
ability to change the circumstances. country
filled a void in my mom's life. Because of her
abuse, she wanted love and someone to lift

her up and make her feel good. So when country did those things, she was blind to the abuse. That had to be why she stayed with him for 31 years. He filled her holes. He abused her verbally, by manipulating and putting her down. He played off her emotional holes. He came in and made her feel wanted, with control. He manipulated her and filled those holes that were super deep. In one breath he told her she was a great woman, then in the next breath he tore her down and made her feel like she wasn't good enough. He even impregnated another woman while married to my mother.

I remember she called me while I was at SU. I could tell it hurt her tremendously, although she acted as if she didn't care. She told me the baby's mother kept calling the house. I could hear the pain in her voice. But she stayed. She decided to change her number. This was sort of like when my mom

decided to put a lock on my door. She
thought that would keep him out. Funny stuff
huh? All these Band-Aids but never really
healing the situation at its core. country
smothered my mother, he didn't allow her to
go places without him, and he was super
controlling. There were times I wanted to see
her and when I expressed that, she
responded with hesitation because he didn't
like her to be without him. And there was no
way I was going to be around him.
Whenever I was around him a sharp
negative energy would shoot through my
body. It didn't feel good at all. Of course, I
didn't know my power either. I didn't know
how to be close to my mother and still value
how I felt at that time. I didn't know how to
balance.

I wonder how my mother felt knowing her
husband was sexually abusing her daughter,
flirting with females in her face, and getting

another woman pregnant. There were many times my mom had the choice to experience happiness. I learned that her heart broke the first day he touched me. She knew what it felt like. She didn't know how to save me and how to make a huge change like that. Because she experienced abuse, and thought she was OK, she thought I would be also.

She was sent several exit strategies. But she couldn't see. *If you can't see the life jackets being thrown to you, how could you put one on?* That's how I know that this was her lesson to learn and her life path. She had choices. She had to want change badly enough that she could overcome her greatest fears. I learned that her road had to be travelled just the way it did. However, I wasn't OK.

I know I went through something that millions of people have gone through and are still experiencing. I also know that God put a fire in me to affect change. I look at my life as a testimony so that I can hopefully help someone get through their tests. Change is a very tough thing to do. It may be the hardest thing to do when you have been abused. The patterns we develop to protect ourselves become habits almost impossible to break. Then when you add fear, change seems even more scary and unattainable. We have to remember that God is love and would not dangle strong feelings of possibility if there wasn't any possibility. Also think about change like this, when you pray for something-change is what you wished for.

Whatever higher power you believe in is always working with us, even though we are taught, and usually believe, that things are always working against us. But that's not true. Fear of change is just another veil

JAI HUDSON

keeping us away from the prize — which is ultimate self-love.

MORE UNVEILING

Because of my challenges, I developed my voice. I was able to finally get it all out. No more stomach pains, no more lumps in my throat, and no more eczema. It's funny that as soon as I changed my perception and released all of the emotions tied to my abuse, I felt so much lighter and my health got better.

Through my pain I gained a certain type of strength. The best way to describe it is I feel spiritually powerful and invincible. I finally learned what it means to love myself. Subconsciously I was blaming myself for what happened to me. I hated my beauty because I felt that caused my abuse. I hated how I was because obviously I caused this to happen. I spent so much time feeling

JAI HUDSON

unworthy, and expressing love to everyone except me. I became so empty emotionally. I had to fill up fast. I needed to start the process of Self-love.

Maybe my mom wished the whole thing would disappear. Or that he'd disappear. I will never really know for sure. I do know that my mother loved me. I just didn't know how to love me. And I do know that my mother admired my strength, the power to stand up for my beliefs. She knew I would be OK even after the abuse. She also relied upon me to do something to affect change. She had a lot of faith in me. In the midst of all the pain and negativity there were the many gifts of **Grace.**

JAI HUDSON

XVIII

LESSONS

JAI HUDSON

"GOOD LIFE"

Song By KANYE WEST

Welcome to the good life
Where niggaz that sell D
Won't even get pulled over in they new V
The good life, let's go on a living' spree
Shit they say the best things in life are free
The good life, it feel like Atlanta
It feel like L.A., it feel like Miami
It feel like N.Y., summertime Chi, ahh (Now throw
your hands up in the sky)
So I roll through good
Y'all pop the trunk, I pop the hood, Ferrari
And she got the goods
And she got that ass, I got to look, sorry
Yo it's got to be cause I'm seasoned
Haters give me them salty looks, Lowry's
50 told me go 'head switch the style up
And if they hate then let 'em hate
And watch the money pile up, the good life
Now I, I go for mine, I got to shine
Now throw your hands up in the sky
Now I, I go for mine, I got to shine
Now throw your hands up in the sky
Imma get on this TV mama, Imma
Imma put shit down
Hey, hey, hey, hey, hey, hey
Hey, I'm good

JAI HUDSON

ACCEPT YOUR EXPERIENCES

I learned that my mother knew her husband had an addiction. He was born in South Carolina and confided in my mother the reason why he left. He left because he raped his ex-wife's niece. My mother knew this and yet still allowed him to be around her child. I learned this information after my mom passed and after I forgave her husband. Would things be different if I knew he had a record of abusing females? Life unfolds in mysterious ways. So the abuse I endured could have been prevented? How would life be different? Would I be different? *So many questions-with no possible way of knowing the answers.* I know one thing for sure and that is I would not have the strength and wisdom I have today if I didn't go through my set of experiences. After finding out this information, instead of being angry I saw things super clear.

I saw that my intuition was right on point way back when I was two years old. I felt something even then, like I somehow knew country was a monster. I saw why I didn't know this information growing up. Imagine how difficult that would have been, knowing my mother knew he was a pedophile early in their relationship. The extra dysfunctions and anger I would have had inside too, if I had known. I also saw that my mom tried to forgive him as God had forgiven her. This is deep stuff, I know. It took a lot of growth, unconditional love, patience with myself and others, music, and conversations with God to get me here.

FACING FEARS

I had to face my fears head on. As I did, I realized that things are usually not as bad as I thought. Anything is overcome-able. Who was the monster I had been running from for so long?

According to the Psychology Today article titled, "All about Fear:" "Fear is a vital response to physical and emotional danger — if we didn't feel it, we couldn't protect ourselves from legitimate threats. But often we fear situations that are far from life-or-death, and thus hang back for no good reason. Traumas or bad experiences can trigger a fear response within us that is hard to quell. Yet exposing ourselves to our personal demons is the best way to move past them."

1 John 4:18 — *There is no fear in love. But perfect love drives out fear.*

I learned that fear is merely the "closest opposite" of love. If you don't love there has to be some kind of fear-based emotion involved. That's what I believe. Fear kept me from love, faith, growth, self-love, forgiveness, confidence, standing in my own power and so much more. At the end of the day everyone just wants love. I feared disappointment so I didn't acknowledge something so vulnerable as wanting love. We remain quiet because we fear not being believed or of the outcome. We don't face ourselves because we fear the unknown. *Fear, fear, fear.*

   country feared my mom and I. He feared the power and love we had between us. Because of that, he manipulated her and tried to control us. My mom feared losing her husband and what she thought was love. That's how life is, we each have different perceptions of what love feels like; we each have different fears. We each experience different expressions of love as we grow up. My mom never dealt with her pain. So she was in a relationship where she couldn't see

JAI HUDSON

the dysfunctions as deal breakers because she had endured pain so much greater. She became a melting pot of fear and pain.

The spoken and unspoken mantra passed along from generation to generation in my family was, "You'll be OK." But I wasn't and my mom sure wasn't. And you're not OK after you've been abused. My family feared judgment, change, and truth. But life's hard places don't disappear just because we don't want to deal with them. Life's ruthless like that. The only opposition in life is self. So when we fear people, places and things, we are truly fearing something regarding self. I am not talking about fears of an abuser. I am talking about the fears within. If it scares you, face it! If it makes you uncomfortable, explore it! Believe me, it's only scary because it's a new way of being. We are the questions and the answers. The alpha and omega. Healing starts and ends with self.

JAI HUDSON

YOU ALWAYS HAVE THE POWER

Even with all the things that happened, I still had the power! I always had it. country tried to take that power away. The power I was given by God. How could he possibly think he could do that? I had to make the decision for myself to leave. I had to put myself first. At the time I didn't know that's what I was doing. But if my mother wasn't going to stand up, I had to. I always had the power. Sexual abuse and molestation almost always is about control and power over another. Manipulation and Fear are used to psychologically rape the mind of the victim, leaving the abused feeling low emotionally. The goal of the abuser is to feed their disease by making the victim feel they are powerless. But if you never had any power, then why is the abuser manipulating you at all? Why does the abuser need to control

JAI HUDSON

you? Ding-ding-ding! That's right, because you *do* have a power. You are a light they are trying to dim.

It seemed like my challenges were designed for me to give up, stay quiet, and be powerless. First the sexual abuse, then my mom not protecting me, then his way of controlling my mom and I, having the decision of whether he stays or leave, my sister crying for her father, being told to keep things a secret, my mom telling me she can't afford to send me to college, losing my mother, and so much more. But I beat the odds. I didn't give up. I didn't stay quiet either, even with the guilt of leaving. Even though I didn't know that's what I was doing. I did not give up. I followed my heart from day one.

When I think back, there were little whispers guiding me through life, showing me the way. That's how life is too. We all

JAI HUDSON

receive those messages guiding us through life. Not just me. I got out of that house and God blessed me with the ability to see the world. He showed me that the life I experienced in my mother's household was not the be all and end all to life. I had options and a chance at true happiness.

It's a huge task to attempt to change a planet, however it's much easier to change self. Situations will change if you change how you perceive them — that's a fact. I had to change my perception of the pain I experienced. I started to think, *what if I went through this abuse to truly understand and help someone younger or even older heal from his or her abuse? What if that was the only reason I experienced abuse at all?* Going from being a *victim* to being *victorious*. That's how I started to look at my situation. I wanted to see a purpose for my abuse, and see the positivity in my pain, stand in my power and take my power back.

We have to recognize the power we have. Yes, even us who have been abused. That makes us even more special. We have experienced pain but we are still here with the ability to heal. Some don't have that option. Because God doesn't give us more than we can handle, we can heal and rise above our circumstances. Know your worth, recognize your power, and stand in it. Standing in your power is directly linked to following your heart.

POWER OF VOICE

Maya Angelou's "I know why the caged bird sings" had a major effect on me. She spoke up regarding her abuse. Her abuser was put in jail and then killed. She felt her voice got him killed so she stopped speaking for six years. My situation was very different. I told my mom about my abuse and nothing was done. I began to feel my voice wasn't important or valued. When I first read that book I identified with Ms. Angelou so much. I could totally see how a person could lose their voice or not speak up.

I always felt like my mom had her family with my sister and her father. The abuse I endured from her husband made me feel excluded. I wasn't part of their family because I was different. I couldn't be quiet about my abuse. I couldn't sweep that under the rug. I couldn't keep the pain I felt a secret. I couldn't pretend that we were one big happy family. I could not allow him to think it was OK.

For years I've had the same recurring dream. I mean, I have lots of dreams, but this one always stands out, but never seemed important or interesting enough to tell someone about. Within the dream I can't speak. It was like there was cotton in my mouth. During the dream, I am trying desperately to get this foreign object out of my mouth so I can talk and breathe freely. This usually happened when I wanted to say something to someone. However, I couldn't get any words out. It was so weird. I attempted to remove the cotton out of my mouth but I could never completely get all of it out. It seemed to never end. In the dream, this is all happening in front of the person I want to express myself to. Sometimes it was my mother, sometimes it was a significant other, and sometimes it was country and his family. I dreamed of telling my family how he abused me, and the reason I stayed away from the family. I didn't know if not being able to speak in the dream was a sign to be quiet or to speak up. So I never said anything.

JAI HUDSON

This had to be symbolic. One of my issues has been speaking up for myself. Conveying my complete emotion and feelings has been difficult for many years. When I was young, I heard I didn't have that problem. Usually someone was trying to get me to be quiet. Later, the reason I didn't speak up for myself or express complete emotion was fearing the consequences — that I wouldn't be loved. And the other reason I didn't speak up was because it seemed like my voice didn't matter anyway. Remember I told my mother and nothing was done? I now know that I have to stand up and speak out regarding my feelings. We have to stand up no matter what! Speak up, release all fears, and have immense faith in the higher power and ourselves.

JAI HUDSON

HEAL THROUGH CREATIVITY

Douglass Ehy wrote, "So many people experience unwanted sexual contact, rape and other forms of sexual abuse. And they often help deal with the aftermath through creative expression, perhaps using art therapy, but more often some other form of creative self-expression." ("Creative Expression and Sexual Abuse" – Article)

Creativity has always been the driving force in my life, an outlet. I loved everything about art and creative expression. I danced, I sang, I acted, I wrote stories, I created clothing, I created my own Halloween costumes, I was a super visual person even at a young age. Because I wasn't able to express myself verbally and emotionally, I had to find another way. I didn't know what I was doing at the time, but I was healing. To release and let go is a part of healing. Why do you think some of the greatest albums in music are either super creative or express truth or pain? Look at Mary J Blige's *My Life* album, or Michael Jackson *Thriller* — expressions of pain and creativity. Greatness comes from within, and those two emotions are extremely relatable. We all share similar emotions because truth and pain are universal. Creativity is such a powerful tool in healing. Creativity can be anything. Writing is healing. As I said earlier, I had to quiet my mind as much as possible. I used music, however for you it may be painting, cooking, singing — whatever calms your soul. This is truly a powerful way to use your power and voice.

TURN PAIN INTO PROGRESS

After the abuse happened, different scenarios played in my head. Will my family and mother really believe me? Would country hurt us? It's such a scary place to be and especially if you're a child, there are all types of fears that clutter the mind. These fears start to rule your world; they block you from living. I escaped a lot in my mind. That helped me tremendously.

In healing, I practiced being in the moment. When I slowed the world down, I was able to see the many messages sent to me throughout the day. God is always sending messages, answers and guidance. Once I was able to silence the noise around me it became easier to recognize them. Messages show up on television, as contact from someone special just mentioned, on the radio, in the form of repeating numbers, whispers, and etc.

We tend to focus on the pain and anger of a situation, so it's almost impossible to recognize the messages. However, if you are able to focus that energy into something that acts as a release, you can get out of that painful place quicker. My thing was working out, taking a walk, jogging, yoga, getting a tattoo, sports, boxing, writing, dancing, or anything where you can quiet your mind and calm your soul, and focus on you. Once I was able to clear my mind and focus, I asked God questions and paid close attention to the answers sent. Everything we need is always sent to us. Everything! But we have to be quiet enough to recognize the gifts. And if we are experiencing pain and your life is "noisy" how can you truly accept the gifts? How can we recognize the Grace? There's nothing we can't heal from because we always *have Grace.*

MY FEELINGS NOW

Ultimately, I feel like a new person now, having gone through my set of challenges. I learned my worth, how to stand up for myself, trusting my intuition, the strength and

JAI HUDSON

power I possess, the true meaning of faith,
how forgiveness equals freedom, and finally
how to love *me* unconditionally. Motivated by
the residue of abuse and not wanting to
continue the cycle I was going through, I had
to stop running and face my pain. Face my
truth.

I forgave my mom twelve days before
she passed away. I'm so thankful I was
given the chance to tell her those special
words and free her from a past of pain and
guilt as it related to me. That was truly a gift
for the both of us. (Sidebar: do you see how
God is always on time?) I am truly blessed. I
was granted the gift of Grace in forgiveness.

I was supposed to know I'm beautiful
inside and out, a human being who
genuinely cares about other people, that I'm
powerful and I have a purpose. I'm a
survivor, and if I negated one event in my
life, I would not be at the exact place, exact

moment, with the lessons I've learned or special people in my life, the accomplishments I've made, or the strength of my faith. Everything would be different. Also, things could have been a lot worse. I accept the cards that were dealt to me.

SELF-LOVE

Abuse depletes the soul. We have to fill ourselves back up. But with what? That's right, *LOVE*. It all stems from lack of self-love, and fear. But what is fear? I've read a ton of books and read a million definitions, and yet the prevailing definition of fear seems to be "lack of LOVE." Fear depletes the soul on a continuous basis. It keeps you away from love. We have to learn to love ourselves because love is the antidote for rising above any pain. We need to love self stronger and teach our children to love self.

JAI HUDSON

Most people say it's a selfish thing to focus on self. Throughout life we have been taught to be self-less. But if we do not love ourselves the most, how can we expect someone to express a genuine love toward us when they don't experience our own self-love. We have to model the love we want. Start treating ourselves with love and compassion. I know to some this may sound too easy and sort of cliché. But you will be surprised how many people lack love of self.

I went through life searching for love in all the wrong places. I wanted people to choose me. I longed for someone to love me and show me, that when it came down to it, they would genuinely care. Then I realized that love was always right inside of me. It's crazy that I only learned this just recently, when my mom passed. I was on the outside of me looking for love that was right there inside of me.

JAI HUDSON

My relationship with God has been very special since I was very young. I just didn't know that's who I was speaking to all this time. All those days I prayed that the abuse would stop, or when I cried myself to sleep, or even when I prayed to the air to make me invisible, I never thought about who I was confiding in or who I was talking to. I thought I was just talking to myself. But I was confiding in God.

Without my faith, my love for God, and those conversations with the air, I don't know how I could have gotten through this. I used to pressure myself to get to a place of self-love faster. I hated the fact that I couldn't love myself as strongly as I loved others. I took my time with others but I rushed things with myself. I'd give my all to the people I loved, but didn't know the first thing about what I wanted. I would wake up in the middle of the night and sit with loved ones in the

ER, but I wouldn't do that for myself — and on top of that, I couldn't allow anyone to do that for me either. I didn't know how to receive. I had to start putting me first. Those old feelings were resurfacing of wanting to feel like I mattered. However, I had to matter to me. That was the most important thing I could do was to start loving me, unconditionally

I am now learning how beautiful, how wonderful I am, how much I do matter, and that I am worthy of all life has to offer. I also learned that I am uniquely made and created to be me: JAI HUDSON. I have a power and special gifts to share with the world.

QUOTE FROM ALBERT EINSTEIN

"Loving yourself is very important for the abused child. It's maybe the hardest thing to do. During this time you require an abundance of love from your parents to even

fully understand what love is and to how to give it as well. But it has to be done. We have to learn how to cut through the feelings of negativity towards ourselves and learn to love self-flaws and all.

This universal force is LOVE. When scientists looked for a unified theory of the universe they forgot the most powerful unseen force.

Love is light that enlightens those who give and receive it. Love is gravity, because it makes some people feel attracted to others.

Love is power, because it multiplies the best we have, and allows humanity not to be extinguished in their blind selfishness. Love unfolds and reveals. For love we live and die. Love is God and God is Love. This force explains everything and gives meaning to life. This is the variable that we have ignored for too long, maybe because we are afraid of

love because it is the only energy in the
universe that man has not learned to drive at
will."– Albert Einstein

FORGIVING YOURSELF

I had forgiven my mom, my abuser, and now
it was time to forgive the person who
endured all this pain and survived. The spirit
who remained positive, hopeful and
continued to dream in the midst of all the
trauma. It was time to forgive myself. Let all
the guilt, fears, and most importantly the
past, go. Accept me flaws and all. Forgive
me for my choices, my treatment towards
myself, and my inability to be compassionate
and patient with me. I forgive you Jai.

PRACTICE III

JAI HUDSON

I REALLY, REALLY LOVE YOU

This exercise really helped me with this healing process of self-love. If you need a little help falling in love with you again, here are a few suggestions. Ask people to write some things they like about you; ask them to go deep and reveal something you may not have known or seen about yourself. Write their words down on post-its and hang them near your mirror as reminders.

Stand in front of the mirror, look into your eyes and say, "I love you (say your name), I love you (say your name), I really, really love you (say your name). Practice this until it becomes natural and you begin to genuinely feel that feeling for yourself. It took me a few months to get there, so be patient. Do this every morning. Make the commitment to yourself. No one can love you like you love you.

QUIETING THE INNER CRITIC

After I discovered core issues and identified what my lessons were, I began to fill the holes with self and God. I started to Love and Trust myself, and I accepted that all things are part of a design to help me reach my potential. Now I could finally quiet that inner critic inside. The inner critic is that voice that goes against the things you know are right for you. It's the voice that sometimes tries to protect, but most often responds with the "little ego" involved. So for example when you said, "I'm going to tell," the inner critic was the voice that said, "No one will believe you." However, the inner critic serves a purpose. What I mean is that sometimes that inner voice acts as protection. For example, when country lied about the person he was or him wanting to adopt me, my inner critic told me he wasn't telling the truth. Those voices protected me from manipulation.

I've learned that we need to quiet that voice. Focus on what you want. Train the inner critic to focus on your wants and not the things you don't want. What do you want the outcome to be? Don't worry about the process. Tell that inner voice thank you for your protection, however it is not needed at this time. Who would you rather figure out the maze of life, your little ego or God? I'd rather God, because he can see farther than I can.

LISTEN TO THE WHISPERS

I felt alone. I didn't know what to do to stop the situation from happening. However, I did. Remember, God gave me everything I needed, along with Grace, to get out of whatever situation I was in. I believe that. I am a dreamer. I watched action movies, wrestling, karate… I loved music and loved to draw… I knew I was special. I know I didn't get through as much as I did all alone. I'd receive little nudges and whispers in the form of strong feelings about things, like when I first met my abuser. Sometimes the whisper would be a sick feeling in my stomach. That was "intuition." Or when I was magically guided to live with Talia and her family. At first I thought I was being rebellious, but no, it was "the whispers" again. At the time, I didn't know it was God but now I know I was never alone and you aren't either. Quiet the noise around you and follow the whispers, signs and messages. They are always happening around you.

JAI HUDSON

"GOD DOESN'T GIVE YOU MORE THAN YOU CAN HANDLE"

I know everyone has heard this popular saying. It's true! I remember hearing this as a child and thinking that it was some church lady's motto being repeated over and over, and I never really applied it to my own life. So I'm asking you to think about it and apply it to your life. *Picture yourself as the leading character in an action film. Make that an action star in a blockbuster film. Say you're Zoe Saldana in Columbiana or Neo in The Matrix. Now, if you're Zoe, your character has two hours of ups and downs, your parents killed in front of you, you're born into a life of crime, your grandmother and uncle are murdered in your kitchen, you are shot and have to fight men twice your size. Zoe's life is like a roller coaster ride. However in the end she gets the villains back and is victorious. She always had what she needed to defeat the villains. Whether it was a disguise to get out of harm's way, or a hairpin to escape a jail cell, or the code phrase for vicious Rottweiler's to protect her from the killers, she had everything she needed. If she didn't know how to get through something, God sent someone who did.*

OK, now think of Neo in The Matrix. He always had the power because he was considered "the one" to save the real world. However, he didn't believe it for himself. He faced several battles with machines and robots and also jumped out of a helicopter to save Morpheus. He still didn't believe. He was shot and everyone, including the machines, thought he was dead. However, because he was "the one," he healed himself and rose like Jesus. Now he believed. His power was revealed to him, he was able to stop the flow of bullets coming towards him, and saved the real world from the machines and virtual world. He was given everything he needed, but he also had to believe in himself.

That's what I mean when I say we have everything we need right inside of us. And if we don't have it, better believe it will be provided for you. You also have to be quiet enough to recognize and receive the gifts. Think about your life. Although it may have been painful, can you remember hearing the little whispers, or receiving a magical exit strategy to escape the pain? Or maybe it came in the form of a passion or excitement for something? These things are like life jackets to keep us from drowning. In the heat of the moment we don't recognize them as a saving Grace. But they are. We have the power to get through anything. We just have to listen and believe.

JAI HUDSON

PRACTICE IV

JAI HUDSON

EXERCISE FOR BEING IN THE MOMENT

I've discovered a number of different ways to practice being in the moment. This is one I enjoy, inspired by Stuart Wilde:

Find an ant and follow it. Look at nothing but the ant. Travel with the ant as it scurries along feeling its way to its destination. Notice how the ant is faced with many obstacles along its path — cracks in the road, soil and plants in between the pavement, or a small pebble that's boulder-size to the ant. Pay close attention to how the ant gets past the obstacles. Do this for as long as you have time for. With this practice you are being "in the moment." When we "control time" in this way, we can free ourselves from outside confinements and learn how to quiet our

JAI HUDSON

minds and focus on self. This exercise helps the mind function at a more peaceful level.

In addition, we can imagine being more like the ant, observing how obstacles don't stop the ant, and they don't need to stop us!

XIX

GIFTS OF GRACE

"BEST FRIEND"

Song by MISSY & AALIYAH

I'll still be there for you
In your time of need
You can lean on me
Come on
I'll be there for you

I'll be there for you
In your time of need
You can lean on me
Come on
I'll be there for you

GIFTS

God gave me an outlet in my best friend
Talia Parkinson and her mother Sonia
Anderson. I also received Grace when I
started working with Misa Hylton. She and
her family surrounded me with a love and
protection I needed. Then there's Walter, we
call ourselves twins-because we connected
from the beginning. He was placed in my life
for so many reasons. The Hotboyz, Q
Hardy, Ariane Davis, Wouri Vice, Clarence
Cannon-I have so many people who inspire
me to keep going. Angels sent from God-my
gifts of Grace. Basketball, music, designing
for Missy Elliott and Super Bowl, my many
experiences through work, travelling the
world, meeting Pharrell, my friends in
Brooklyn and Harlem, working with Lil Kim
and Mary J Blige, my imagination, my best
friends and life coaches, my many
relationships, the air I breathe — are just

JAI HUDSON

some examples of Grace. There are so
many gifts of Grace. But I think you get the
point.

One day I learned in coaching and
Shaman healing that hard work isn't
necessary for blessings, or light, or even
love. That's what Grace is — a gift, just
because. I hope after reading my story and
experiencing my journey to where I am now,
you can take away some wisdom and
hopefully see that life's curveballs are
preparation for a life of abundance. Bad or
good, everything happens for a reason and if
you can look at each situation as a chance
to grow internally, you can start to live a
more abundant life. We prevent this from
happening sooner because we tend to hold
on to emotions that no longer serve our
greater good. We have to let go so we can
be free.

JAI HUDSON

Abuse is painful and life-altering. In some cases, people never recover from it. I want to help change that. There are two options after you have suffered abuse. You can be quiet about it and go through life running from emotions, blaming the world and yourself, and living your life from a suffering perspective. You can be mad at the world and continue the cycle that most likely was set in motion by a previous generation, never truly experiencing happiness and ruled by fear.

The other option is to accept, appreciate, and truly understand that everything in your path was designed for you to achieve perfection. It's kind of like roadblocks. The obstacles are only there to be overcome. You know the saying, "Play the cards you're dealt." When we look at life this way, huge mountains become overcome-able obstacles. Life is like a game in that way. It's sort of like chess. You have everything you need on that board. It's all about how you react to opposition and how you utilize your challenger to your benefit.

Visualize where you want to be internally and as a person. If we can start to grasp the idea that every event in your life has a purpose toward reaching your higher self, then this is when you can truly understand what life is about. If you can accept this same idea for another living person, you can start to see the blessings in every situation. Even the abuser involved — forgive them. I know this is difficult. But if I told you happiness is waiting at the end of the road would it make it easier to let go of the pain? Holding on to pain hinders your growth and really doesn't matter at the end of the day. It's like carrying 100, 20-pound bags up and down a series of steep mountains in 122 degree weather. *Why?* Put the load down;

JAI HUDSON

it's much easier to climb the mountains hands-free.

Our personal triumphs are always part of a bigger picture. One thing about *us* who were abused is that we don't wish this on anyone. But what if the abuse you suffered was to show you how to help a child get through their abuse? With that experience we can be the best teachers and protectors. We can change the world.

I needed to try hard to slow it all down. The world, my thoughts, my feelings, my mind... *everything.* I had held my breath since my abuse. I needed to breathe, relax, and just focus on me and what was happening to me. So I did just that. It's like stepping out of your body and looking at yourself. Like really giving yourself 100% attention. We spend so much time trying to get over everything, getting through it and stressing over life. When we look at

JAI HUDSON

ourselves and slow it all down, we are actually loving ourselves. Have you ever hugged and kissed yourself? Have you ever been in love with you? When we focus on ourselves that's exactly what we are doing. We are putting ourselves first.

Let's go back to innocence, the time before any of the veils, holes, or abuse. *That moment when the sun shined the brightest.* Think about it and write it down. Reminisce and try to feel when things were innocent. When all the things we worry about never mattered. Here's my memory of innocence:

Walking out of my building 1865 Fulton with Naquan (my godbrother) to the playground, playing basketball and learning the latest b-ball tricks and moves from the older boys in the park, climbing trees with my cousin James, playing Double Dutch with the girls as the boys interrupted for our attention, sitting and eating in the kitchen

with my great grandma Mama King as she
told me stories of growing up in Barbados
and Brooklyn in the early 1920s, hanging
with my best friend Niesha at the midget
league basketball games and flirting with the
boys, going with my great grandma to the
live chicken market to get fresh meat for
dinner, having my first fight with Lamecka
"Moomoo" in front of PS 21, writing songs
and rapping on my stoop with my best friend
Jay Hitch, competing and winning dancing
competitions, dancing backup for Big Daddy
Kane at Boys & Girls High school African
Day Festival, walking to Carvel with my god
brother and buying orange sherbet ice
cream, rushing home to watch Michael
Jackson's new video, watching the making
of Thriller 22 million times, writing a letter to
TLC to tell them how much they influenced
me, watching "A Different World" and
wishing I could attend Hillman College,

JAI HUDSON

dreaming of becoming a rapper like MC Lyte, Queen Latifah and Left Eye, watching my mother smile and seeing the smile in her eyes.

This was innocence for me. We all have some special moments of innocence. Now, by changing our perspectives, we will create a new innocence. *If God spoke over us, and has a design for us, then external opposition is just part of the design.* We always have what we need to get through anything. That's what Grace is. It's just designed that way. We only have to wake up to recognize it.

GRACE IN NUMBERS

When people say or think they were a mistake, I truly can't agree with that. Even with the situation of rape. I believe we are all created from a thought or with purpose. I also believe the thought of our creation is beyond our parents. What I mean is I feel our creation goes beyond a simple act of sexual intercourse. Nothing is coincidence, so how can someone be a mistake? And If everything happens for a reason and if God puts certain people in our lives for a reason, then we are all created for a reason. I believe we are gifts to our parents, to our families, to the world, straight from the source — God. Everyone is a teacher. We are Grace for others, for the world and for ourselves. That means we are created exactly how we are as a gift. As Oprah Winfrey's says, *"**It's the gift in us that keeps on giving.**"*

I want to thank God for all my instances of Grace. I want to thank you my source for **my mother Donna Elcock and father Richard Washington. Mama King, Dwayne Elcock, James, Lillian Wiltshire, St Clair Elcock, my uncles, music, Wendy King, Byron King, Auntie King, Carolyn**

"Ann" McCoy, Shaneck Holloman thank
you for always being there, Patricia
Holloman, Andrew and Aaron Lord,
Anthony and Andrew, Debra Banks,
Johnny Banks, Naquan Banks, Larry
Banks, Johnesha Banks, Niesha
Johnson, Ronnie and Kermit, James,
Cousin Chrissy Thank you, Pacific Day
Care Center, Leotta Green, my nephew
Nathaniel "BooBoo," Brevoort Housing,
PS 21, Talisha Martin, Roslyn Smallwood,
Shakim Saddler thank you for your
unconditional love, Trevor Diggs and
family, Leroy, Moo-Moo, Shaquanna
Brown, Angel Brown and family,
Charlene and Mary from PS 21, Barbizon,
Mrs. Vicky, Queenie, Mrs. McCoy, Haj
Chinzera Pinnock and her parents,
Bainbridge Street, my 6th grade teacher
Ms. Williams for believing in me, my Ace
Clarence Cannon Jr. I'm so grateful you

entered my life at 13 years old, I love you
beyond thank you for always being my
rock, IS 308, Michael Payton, Paul Cain,
John "Fabolous," Michael Tucker, Trevor
Diggs, Danielle Moore, Melissa
Strickland, Joycetta Ray, Jamiylah
Cooper, Simmone Simmons, James,
Aaron, Timera and Tiersa Flood, Malyka,
Michelle, Tenisha, James, Aaron,
everyone at 308, Talia Parkinson, Sonia,
Alisha, Island of Jamaica, HSTAT, Coach
D, Kiwan Anderson, Mr. Weinberg thank
you for the introduction to books, Ms.
Monaco, Nikia, Ngozi, Tamara, Latoya,
Illustrious "Lus" Greatmind Salley my
heart, Heavenly Salley and family,
Monique Bell, Walter Steele and his
amazing family, Syracuse University,
Alpha Kappa Alpha Sorority Inc., A@A,
DST, Qs, Kappa's, Zetas, SGRhos,
Cortina, Bandit, Marsha Style, Rodetta,

Dionnee, Shauntay, Jason Hart, Randy
Tejeda, Fashion dept. at SU, Keith
Wooten, Dorian Dade (RIP), my spirit twin
Q "LoveBug" Hardy I love you, Jane
Blaze thank you, Kendell, Lizbeth,
Kimbre, Tanisha, Rockwilder, Jay Difeo,
Misa Hylton thank you for being at the
gateway of the biggest moments of my
life I love You, Ariane Davis my
bestfriend thank you for all your love,
Chyna Doll Enterprises the most
incredible school of life for me, Tiffany
Harris, Kenny Carmen, Trena B Real,
Wouri Vice, Aaron Pope, Mariel Haen,
Justin Combs, Niko Brim, Madison Star
Brim, Mimi Chrissy, Cousin Linda,
Jasmine, Gia, Migo, Mimi Janice, Pastor
P, Kelly, Dream, Jasmine, Jazzy, Kelsie,
Bria, Mustafa Hooten and family, Uncle
Daniel (RIP), Aunt Lynda, Hillary Weston,
Eula Myers & Family, Heavy D, Bharat &

family, Kim Snow, Rahlo, Reemo, Sha,
Will, my artists SNL-Shaquille Townsend,
Trey Livingston you 2 are the future I
love you both, VI my bro, Brinz, Jeff,
Vincent Harris, Amari & Brandon, Nonnie,
Quick, Reka Brim, Tiana, Medina, Booka,
Jojo Brim, basketball, Cynthia Alvarez,
Lorena Rios, Emily B, Christian Combs,
Kai, Rashon, TankGod, Tizz, Amani,
Diamond, AJ Brewington, Tasha, (Jackie
Washington from "Jackies Back" movie
lol, David, Seandon, Dashir, Zerick,
Jamie, Lorenzo. Tavon, Darrelle (RIP),
Tavon (RIP), Greg Walker, Berto, Adrian,
Joel (RIP), Marcus, Rich, Richie, AD
Anthony Hemingway, Carlos, Emmanuel,
Jaron, my Hotboyz family thank you for
your love and protection, The Milan
family, Atiba, Roger, Eric, Corey, Larry,
all the BratPack, Kim Snow thank you for
always championing me, snails, Nicole

Marzan, Christina Rice, Trevor Julien,
Tiana Marie, Terrence Davidson,
Seannita Palmer, King magazine, Datwon
Thomas I admire you so much, Art,
Dance, Ariel, Hollis, Tracey Waples, June
Ambrose; Unique London, Rocsi Diaz,
BET, MTV, My Super Sweet 16 show, 106
& Park, Own, HGTV, E TV, Revolt, Vice,
ARTISTS: Heavy D, Eddie F, Queen
Latifah, LB Thank you, Naughty by
Nature, Hype Williams, F Gary Gray, Jada
Pinkett, Angela Bassett, Will Smith,
Michael Jackson, Janet Jackson, Luther
Vandross, Whitney Houston, Puff Daddy
Sean Combs (Thank you for creating a
music movement and opening your home
to me), BadBoy Entertainment, Mark
Pitts, Notorious BIG, Lance "Un" Rivera,
D-Roc, Prince, Lauryn Hill, Tupac,
Aaliyah, TLC, Left Eye, BBD, Salt n Pepa,
Missy Elliott thank you so much for

everything, Mary J Blige you kept me
dreaming thank you, Monica, Beyoncé
Knowles, Kelly Rowland, Destiny's Child,
De La Soul, Timberland, Tribe Called
Quest, Jay Z, Rocafella Records, Brandy,
Lauryn Hill, Aerosmith, MC Lyte, Aaliyah,
Erykah Badu, Monica, Goapele, Diana
Ross, Tracey Ross, Evan Ross, Angela
Bassett, Tracey Morgan, Dougie Fresh,
Slim and Tripps, Kanye West, Faith
Evans, Wutang, Naughty by Nature,
Yoyo, Dre Dre, Snoop Dog, Busta
Rhymes, Total, Lil Kim, Junior Mafia,
Fergie, Kirk Franklin, Teyana Taylor
thank you showing me dreams do come
true, Pharrell Williams for seeing me,
Pusha T, The Clipse, Alicia Keys, Swizz
Beats, DMX, Tamar Braxton, Toni
Braxton, KrisKross, Big Daddy Kane,
Jermaine Dupree, Remy Ma, Papoose,
Trina the rapper, Tweet, The Beatles,

Tina Turner, Mariah Carey, Trey Songz,
Run DMC, 50 Cent, Eminem, NWA,
Game, Foxy Brown, Eve, Naomi
Campbell, Sha money XL, Chris Lighty,
James Cruz, Divine Day, WhooKid, Mona
Scott, Karen Body, Keon, Yandy, Laurie
Dobbins, Olivia Longott, Halim Rice,
Vincent Hurbert, Kirk Burrows, HOV, Dion
Stewart, Brionne "BJ Everett" Everett I
believe in you, Diamond Bailey, Octavia,
Dice 4-5-6, Delores "Chinky" Everett,
Lateesha Everett, Princess Vines, Sari
Baez, Chino my love, Prince, Missy,
Isabela I love you, Brittney, KD, NutNut,
JoBlaq, Rob "Faze," 730 products studio,
Valerie Z., Columbia Records, Wok, Maria
B, Angela Simmons, Vanessa Simmons,
Rev Run, Diggy Simmons, Vida Shoes,
Pastry kicks, Jan Harvey, MTV, NYSC,
Seannita Palmer, Camille "CiCi",
Shondra Rimes, Pat Viala, Steve

Auckvision, Kev, Renaldo, Wardell,
MHFA, Chrissy Lampkin, Dawn, Chynae
Campbell, Sabrina, Nikki Barrington,
Kennise, Madison, Porcha, Mecca Moore,
Soraya, Tammy Ford, Trevor, Jenna
Tyson, Tammy Delorenzo, Naomi Jonas,
Amanda, Zoe, Stephanie M, Stephanie F,
all MHFA Alumni, Ms Wanda, Ms White,
Alice thank you, JCCA for the Abused,
Chris Chambers, Rae Holiday, Gabriel,
"Sunny Money", Sharaya J, GBaby,
Missy Elliott's amazing dancers,
Tuuuurbo ☺, Glo, Angie Stone, Diany,
Raheem the singer, Soup, Aleesha & the
Tell Someone organization, Dapper Dan,
Guy & Louis, 5001 flavors, Nike, My
teachers- Misa, Nicola, Dr. Sebi, Kurtis
Lee Thomas, Claudia in Sedona, Yoga,
Sedona AZ, Yehuda Berg, The Alchemist,
Don Miguel Ruiz, E. Lynn Harris,
Abraham Hicks, Stuart Wilde, Tim Story,

JAI HUDSON

Daniel Goldman, Oprah Winfrey, Iyanla
Vanzant, Brenee Brown, Eckhart Tolle,
Gary Zukav, Deepak Chopra, Caroline
Myss, Ester Hicks, Wayne Dyer, Mike
Walrond and the FCBC family, Howard
Schultz, Starbucks, T.D. Jakes, Michael
London, Steve Harvey, Tyler the
Hollywood Medium, the many books I've
read, Karl Griggs, Terry McMillian, The
books- Beloved, Power of Now, Things
Fall Apart, To Kill a Mockingbird, Coldest
Winter Ever, Healed with Style & Grace,
Satan, Power to Change Anything, the
Zohar, the Bible, Power of Intention, The
Seat of the Soul, New Earth-Awakening
Your Life's Purpose, The Power of Now,
all the beautiful individuals who helped
with production of this book, Misa
(again), Julie Clayton, Latasha Leake,
Sebastian, Quinn, Khalil and his beautiful
mom, Ingramspark, Amazon, Goodreads,

KD, Rob "Faze," Rod Williams, Terron Tidwell, all the people who had anything to do with opportunities I was blessed with, anyone I worked for or with, all the people who helped me or even challenged me to be greater, and anyone who is an extension of these gifts of Grace. I want to thank Brooklyn, Queens, and Harlem, New York City, Los Angeles, Miami for caring for me during my travels and stays. To the Angels I may have missed, you are always in my heart and never forgotten. "This is a God Dream, This is a God Dream, This is Everything... Everything!.... – Kanye West.

XX

I LOVE BEING ME

JAI HUDSON

"FEELS SO GOOD"

Song by BRANDY

I've Been Waiting I Don't Have To Wait No More
Found What I Was Looking For
With You I Will Spend My Life Standing By Your Side
No More, Lonely Nights At Home
Sitting By The Telephone
Now That I Have You, I Wont Let You Go
I Will Give You All Of Me Baby
You Make Me Feel So Good
I Always Knew You Would Touch My Spot, Make Me
Hot All Over
You Make Me Feel So Good
I Always Knew You Could
Be The One To Give Me Some
I Need It Now
It Feels So Good

INTUITION AND EMOTIONS

It wasn't until I was able to connect my strong intuition to my emotions that I was able to let go of the self-judgment. Intuition also appears to be influenced by awareness and understanding of emotions. I have included an excerpt here, written by Sherrie Dillard entitled, "Your Intuitive Connection to Love." I think this article explains intuition and emotions perfectly.

'Love and intuition seem to go together like peanut butter and jelly, the sun and the moon, and...well, like two people in love. Who at one time or another has not felt a shiver move up their spine or their stomach leap in joy when looking into another's eyes? Have you ever met someone and instantly felt a connection with them or somehow knew what they were thinking or feeling, without knowing how you knew? These are spontaneous natural occurrences of intuition and they can be so commonplace we often take them for granted.

We all have innate intuitive ability, which can be as simple as knowing something without knowing how you know it. Yet intuition, like love, can be mysterious and compelling and can bypass the rational and logical. This is because both love and intuition have their roots in the soul — the deeper, wiser part of us. They are both powerful energies that can enhance every aspect of your life. Knowing one will gain you instant access into a better understanding of the other.

"Your intuition is as unique as you. I have discovered through many years of teaching others to access and develop their innate intuitive ability that intuition surfaces in four primary ways. You may receive energy information through your thoughts, your emotions, your energy field, or your physical body. These four different intuitive modalities make up your intuitive type.

"If you intuit mostly through your thoughts and ideas, you are a mental intuitive. Mental intuitives are naturally "telepathic." Telepathy is the ability to tune into, receive, and send thought messages to another or a group. Emotional intuitives intuit mostly through their emotions. If you tend to easily pick up on others' feelings, are empathetic and tend to be the go-to person for your friends and family who are in need of a kind shoulder, you are likely an emotional intuitive. Spiritual intuitives receive intuitive vibrations through their energy field. Those who can perceive angels and "auras" have an active dream life and enjoy daydreaming may be spiritual intuitives. Physical intuitives absorb energy information into their body. Do you ever feel others' aches and pains or feel flushed and warm just sitting next to certain people? If so, you may be a physical intuitive.

"Once you are aware of your intuitive type, you will be able to develop and use your natural intuition with more ease and success. Your intuitive type also plays an important part in your ability to communicate, understand, and increase intimacy with loved ones." (From an article written by Sherrie Dillard, "Your Intuitive Connection to Love.")

God created me with the superpower of being able to feel deeply. Emotions are superpowers. I've grown up afraid to let my emotions rule me, fearing I might end up somewhere I wouldn't be able to come back from, like my father. However, being emotional and feeling things deeply helped me understand my intuition.

JAI HUDSON

FILLING MY HOLES WITH ME

I did not like people to look at my abuse as a reason for who I was. I was a tomboy and played sports, but was that because of the effects of violation from a man? I didn't want to accept that. And although that had truth to it, It was not the complete me. God created me with all my unique qualities before I met my abuser. When I covered up physically with baggy clothes — that was a survival tactic. I had created it and other survival tactics as a "shield" to protect myself. I don't have to protect myself from country anymore. That time is over and long gone. I let the outside world and my problems steer me away from the gift of my imagination. My imagination is a part of my gift. Exploring my creativity through my imagination kept me alive. All the nights I felt like ending my life quickly changed into visions of me on stage. Dreaming was the driving force that kept me

JAI HUDSON

from giving up. It also prevented me from becoming my circumstances. I was discouraged from loving that about me because others didn't do the same thing. I was a black sheep because I was different. However, I had to start to embrace my gift. Accept it. Fall in love with it.

I used to pretend around certain people. Trying to appear more feminine or being "surface" because that's what "normal" women did. I judged myself so harshly and felt like I couldn't be me. Being me wasn't good enough and I was so different from the norm. I became very quiet, didn't really like club parties, wasn't into hard party drugs, didn't have a high heel fetish, material things weren't important to me, the music industry lifestyle just didn't excite me, and I loved being in monogamous relationships.

During my 20s, I started to think something was really wrong with me. I

JAI HUDSON

remember researching introverts because I had heard I was an introvert: "a shy, reticent person." I could relate to the meaning, but then I got mad because I didn't want to be called an introvert either. *Damned if you do damned if you don't*, right?

I looked up the meaning of introvert: "Introverts tend to look within for answers versus having the need for societal approval. The introvert will stand his or her ground with complete disregard for how others perceive him or her. If you are an introvert, then you will find complete comfort in solitude. You often find yourself immersed in deep thought and contemplation. Your need for approval by others is significantly less than the extrovert as you realize that all answers come from within. While you may partake on social occasions, you often enjoy simply watching the environment around you versus being the center of attention, which many introverts try to avoid. On a metaphysical level, the introvert realizes how we are all connected and does not need the external approval and attention that is often sought by the extrovert. Approximately 75% of the world are extroverts, which makes the introvert the minority, yet the introvert will not succumb to societal pressure in order to conform."

Wow, that was deep. I had to look at things differently because God created me for a reason. I'd tell my friends that all the time, so I needed to take my own advice. All the qualities I once thought were negative or flaws began to look like gifts. I started to be OK with being an introvert. It felt better for me to be in my peaceful apartment looking out my window staring at the New York skyline, creating magic through art. I didn't want to be popping bottles at the after-party. I didn't want to wear heels that hurt, just to impress guys. I wanted guys to like me for me. I didn't want give myself away sexually to random people. To each is own. But I didn't want these things. I had another dream. It became easy to fall in love with me when I realized I was created exactly the way I am for a greater reason.

I had taken my power back at this point. Looking at all the things I once perceived as not so good things, as positives and motivators for my journey of growth is how I filled my holes with me. Owning your power lies in how you view the situation. As soon as you take the pain and hurt out, you strip the opposition of any power they had over you. Yup, it's that simple. Don't you want to go through your baggage now rather than later? Get it over with? Face it now so you can live a life of freedom and abundance with no attachments bringing you down?

JAI HUDSON

Start with all the things swirling around in your mind right now, the things you relate to within my story. If anything you heard triggers a feeling in your stomach, start with those things first. There's a reason for those emotions inside of you. Once you open yourself to the healing process, the path will reveal itself. God will show you the way. So, you don't have to even think of what's going to happen. Remember, no fear. You were built for whatever is in your path. There's nothing really that shocking, or scary, for that matter. We may not like the result but we can get through anything. Look at what we've already accomplished. Look at what we've already experienced. Focus on what you want the outcome to be. Let your intuition guide you.

If you stay in the *great feelings* of what you want to manifest, it's easier for *the great things* to happen. We have to stay in the feeling. Have patience with yourself. The path will have its bumps. But because you are still breathing, change is always possible and beneficial. The rest of your life depends on it. And your children's lives are affected by your life.

I am not saying that what has worked for me will work for you. But I do know that increasing self-love, forgiveness, facing fears, quieting the inner critics, paying attention to your intuition and changing how you view a situation are the ways to begin *any* healing process. These actions free you from holding on to a pain that no longer serves you. And you just might find your holes filling up with the goodness of who you are.

JAI HUDSON

PRACTICE V

JAI HUDSON

TRAIN YOUR MIND

Each day is a new day, and with each new day comes changes and opportunity. Quit dwelling on how things happened before! When you find yourself rehashing something unpleasant from the past, just tell yourself, "Stop it!." The past is gone, done, over with. Cease any worries of what you want the future to be like or not like, too. Our thoughts can develop bad habits too, and like a needle on a scratched record, they can keep repeating the same thing over and over. Sometimes it's easy and effective to simply say "no more." When you interrupt your negative thinking habits, fill that hole by building good habits. Dream your dreams of happiness without restrictions or limitations. What does happiness look like for you? Envision the outcome and forget the process. Embrace the steps to get where

JAI HUDSON

you want to be. Are you on an island basking in the sun? Or maybe traveling to a country you always dreamed of visiting? Or swimming with dolphins in the ocean? Just dream! Don't think about how you will get there. Just smell the ocean, and feel the sun beaming on your skin. This is what life is truly about, the moments when you are happiest and at peace.

HAPPY PLACE

Purchase a journal or writing book, and a candle with a scent that you like. Choose a place where you won't be interrupted and feel the most comfortable — it might be your bedroom, outside in garden, or even in the bathroom — anywhere that you feel a sense of calm. If possible, dim the lights and light the candle.

Sit comfortably and close your eyes. Breathe in through your nose, hold it for six seconds, and release through your mouth. Repeat this twice. Now pay attention to your body. Do you feel a little light-headed? That's the feeling we are aiming for.

With your eyes still closed, envision yourself in a beautiful home — a home that is owned by you. Visualize what it looks like and how it feels to be there. What do you see? What does the décor look like? Does your bedroom overlook the pool, or perhaps you have a sweeping view with trees and mountains in the distance? Continue to dream for as long as you can, adding more and more details to your masterpiece. Remember, you can create whatever you want! These two steps are how you can train yourself to quiet the mind and go into your happy place. This is where you can connect with God, the universe, source, and your angels. These energies are all working together and working with/for you. This is the same place where all your dreams and desires attract manifestation. Remember from physics? — "Like attracts like." This is exactly what this is.

Spend as much time as you can going to this happy place. You are training your mind, freeing your soul, and allowing yourself to be in the energetic space for manifestation.

XXI

PURPOSE

God's Opinion Of Me Makes Man's Opinion Irrelevant

– Tim Story

"I WAS HERE"

Song by Beyoncé

I wanna leave my footprint on the sands of time
know there was something that, and something that I
left behind
When I leave this world, I'll leave no regrets,
Leave something to remember, so they won't forget
I was here I lived, I loved
I was hereI did, I've done, everything that I wanted
And it was more than I thought it would beI will
Leave my mark so everyone will know
I was here
I want to say I lived each day, until I die
And know that I meant something in somebody's life
The hearts I have touched will be the proof that I
leave
That I made a difference, and this world will see

I was here I lived, I loved
I was hereI did, I've done, everything that I wanted
And it was more than I thought it would be
I will leave my mark so everyone will know
I was here I lived, I loved I was here
I did, I've done, everything that I wanted
And it was more than I thought it would be
I will leave my mark so everyone will know
I was here
I just want them to know
that I gave my all, did my best
Brought someone to happiness
Left this world a little better just because I was here
I was here I lived, I loved I was here

JAI HUDSON

I did, I've done, everything that I wanted
And it was more than I thought it would be
I will leave my mark so everyone will know
I was here
(I lived), I lived(I loved), I was here(I did), I did(I've
done), I was here (I lived), I lived (I loved) I was here
(I did), I did (I've done)
I was here

JAI HUDSON

WHY I AM HERE

I've always questioned why am I here.
What's my purpose? God created every
human being with a purpose. Your purpose
is bigger than something you're good at and
are compensated for. God's purpose resides
in the space of joy and happiness. His level
of happiness for us surpasses our own
personal idea of what happiness is. We have
to truly unveil ourselves from the darkness
so we can see the light God instilled in all of
us. I know how difficult it is to be abused and
to clean up the mess left behind. I thought I
was alone. But we are never alone.

My mom left the physical earth at an
early age of 56. I believe she felt she didn't
have the power to change her
circumstances, however, somehow I knew
she believed in me. My greatest blessing is
the relationship I had with my mother in the

early years of my life. I know what real love is because I felt it with my mother. I know what it feels like to care for someone deep to the core.

That's why I wrote this memoir. I feel her passion for me, for using my powers to affect change. I know she wants me to help the abused, and relay to them that they are not alone and there's always a way out.

STYLE AND GRACE

I still can't believe she is gone. I thought she would live forever. I have been a fashion stylist for 14 years, but April 11, 2014 was my greatest styling engagement: I styled my mom for her home-going services. I heard all the wonderful things said by her friends and loved ones at the service. My mother's co-workers and her job meant everything to her. She spent 37 years working there. She went into cardiac arrest at her job. She loved her job. I sat in the front row and listened to her co-workers reminisce about their experiences with my mom. It was such a beautiful feeling to know they loved her almost as much as I did.

During the service my aunt fainted, my uncle was on the verge of having a breakdown, my sister broke down crying, and I consoled them all. I had to be strong. I felt so numb during the funeral. It was like I wasn't there at all. I couldn't believe this day was actually happening. My mother was actually gone. She was laid there in front of me in a pearl white casket. She was dressed in a cream suit, pants and jacket with a white blouse underneath. She also wore a scarf around her neck, as she liked to do. I requested red lipstick because my mother loved one particular photo of her in which she wore red lipstick. She looked beautiful.

JAI HUDSON

My godmother Debra and my sister knew about my abuse, however I only told my uncle and Ann in the hospital, after my mom went into cardiac arrest. So it wasn't a secret anymore. My mother was no longer physically here, and I had kept the secret all this time for her. It was time to let it go.

I felt so weird during the funeral. It was like déjà vu, since I had dreamed of a similar day before. In the dream I couldn't speak. There was a crowd of family members waiting for me to speak and nothing would come out. This day was unfolding exactly as it did in my dreams, however I didn't know in the dream that it was my mother's funeral. In the dream I tried desperately to tell my family how country abused me. However, I never had the chance to tell them because I couldn't speak.

At the funeral, I suddenly stopped consoling my uncle and whispered to my godmother, "I'm going up." I stood up and walked to the microphone.

> *My dear mother.*
> *I love you so much.*
> *No regrets.*
> *Just love. I want to thank everyone for being in her life.*
> *I want to thank her co-workers because she loved them and took her last breath at work. I know I have not been around but I spoke to my mom very often. That was due to circumstances I won't speak of today.*
> *I love you mom and I'm going to miss you.*

When I said *"due to circumstances"* I could see country stand up, as if he wanted to interrupt what he feared was coming — my telling of what he did to me. I didn't even look in his direction; I just put the microphone down and walked down the aisle exiting the church. We laid my mom to rest in Cypress Hills Cemetery, of course, keeping her in her hometown Brooklyn New York. However, she is right by my side everywhere I turn. I can feel her with me all day. I love her so much and miss her terribly.

I have grown so much spiritually and emotionally. I have discovered my power and have begun to truly love Jai and Jacquetta. I hated what being "Jacquetta" felt like because of all the pain I endured during that part of my life. I believe I have finally forgiven myself. I accept and love Jacquetta, pain and all. I legally changed my name in 2007 to Jai Hudson. I didn't identify with the name Jacquetta anymore. It felt confining. Changing my name to Jai, I felt renewed — a survivor.

JAI HUDSON

The name Jai is a Sanskrit name. In Sanskrit the meaning of the name Jai is "victorious." Wow, I had no idea that's what Jai meant when Talia named me back in the day. The name was perfect. If I look back five years, I was nowhere near where I am mentally and spiritually today. It feels like God took over the wheel even though he was always driving, and showed me the way through it all. That magic navigation. I started to recognize that life was bigger than what I knew it to be. I had a bigger purpose and a bigger plan. Life is so much easier to navigate when you let go and let God.

Being given the opportunity to get over your pain is a chance to change and face your fears. Take it. Learn about you and the catalyst to why you do all the things you do. Recognize your gift of Grace. Discover what it is you truly want. Discover you.

JAI HUDSON

You have begun the process of unlocking your gifts of Grace. As you see, Grace is happening all around us. We only have to quiet the world to recognize them. Let's get started!

But of course, let's Heal with Style and Grace.

PASSION

In a society where music is judged, and not seen as a saving mechanism, I want to say that music saved my life. From the very beginning, being exposed to Michael Jackson, Diana Ross, The Beatles, Whitney Houston, Luther Vandross, BBD, TLC, Mary J Blige, Monica, Lauryn Hill, Tweet, Faith, Kanye West, Jay Z, Beyoncé, among so many others, has been a saving Grace for me. The music I most connect with has a message, whether it be about love, how to get through an obstacle, how to become powerful inside, or simply how to have fun.

JAI HUDSON

It's your perception — your interpretation.
Music sometimes mirrors a sense of power
or motivation to never give up and unites all
races, ages, and social classes. Music is so
powerful. Words saved my life and I escaped
through the melodies. I'd get lost in music to
forget the pain. Music is such a beautiful
creation.

"The Weight Of Your Experience Is
Always On You "– JAY Z

"Do you have the power to get up from under
you and be you?" –Jay Z   No longer could I
rely on old gimmicks and tricks to get
through anymore. I had to become an
individual with a deeper meaning to life. I
had to find my passions. I needed to identify
what brought me happy feelings. When did I
feel most powerful? What did I want? What
do I love?

JAI HUDSON

Your passion is something deep inside that you are truly confident about but the fears overshadow. The fears are put in place to keep you from your passion because your passion is directly connected to your purpose. Try to envision what this looks like: If your passion is your heart, then you follow your heart to reveal your purpose. That's how I see it. It's like your passion leads you to your purpose. When you follow what you love you get closer and closer to your purpose. The way you can recognize if you are going in that direction is by the feelings you feel. It's like everything magically appears within you, it feels good and it becomes super clear. It's like the guy in the *Limitless* movie; he magically had all the answers and had tunnel vision to create the life he wanted.

JAI HUDSON

Our lives are just that precious, each and every one of us. Let's lift ourselves to our highest height.

"Always remember deep in your heart that all is well and everything is unfolding as it should. There are no mistakes anywhere, at any time. What appears to be wrong is simply your own false imagination. That's all." ~Robert Adams

Finding your purpose. This is one of those things where you have to rely on intuition and emotions. Being able to quiet the mind is a major prerequisite to listening to your body for direction. Your body and spirit let's you know what your purpose is. It's kind of like the childhood game "hot piece and butter." The closer you get to the hidden object (in reality your purpose) your team screams out that you're hot and getting close. So the closer you get to your purpose your body will let you know. Your purpose is why you are even here on earth. We all have a unique purpose. I realized that my purpose is directly linked to music/creativity, love, and spirituality. I discovered that whenever I think of these things I automatically get happy inside. Love, creativity, and spirituality are the only things that can wake me up from a long overdue sleep or occupy my time with no restrictions. Those specific things speak to my soul. They are my life-lines, which are directly linked to my heart.

PRACTICE VI

JAI HUDSON

FINDING YOUR PURPOSE

Think about what it is that excites your soul. What if I told you that you just won 22 billion dollars? Feel that kind of euphoric feeling. Truly experience what that does to your body and hold on to that feeling. This is the same sensation that living your purpose brings. If your purpose is what you're here to do on the planet, then saying your purpose to yourself should feel like an alignment. It feels like life's meaning is clearer and your place in the world begins to make perfect sense.

Maybe you took ballet as a child, because your purpose is healing through the arts. Or maybe that's why I wrote songs and short stories as a child to escape, because part of my purpose is to write this book to help others heal. And yes, I just got excited as I wrote that last line — I felt the alignment when I spoke my truth about my purpose. Take some time and discover what makes you excited, what feels good, and what gives you "chills" all over your body. That felt-sense is your intuition steering you in the right direction. That's a sacred gift. Intuition is a gift and is always working with you to guide you. Remember the questions and answers to life always end with you.

"LOVE IS ALL WE NEED"

Song by Mary J Blige

Love is All we need
Everybody need love
Love is All we need to make everything complete
If we trying to live together and be happy
You and me are one
And we only just begun
So let's make a new beginning and have some fun
Love is all we need to make everything complete
All we need is L-O-V-E
Love is all we need
Cause everybody needs love

JAI HUDSON

XXII
EPILOGUE
ANGEL OF MINE

JAI HUDSON

FULL CIRCLE

Life has been all I ever dreamed of. Sometimes I have to pinch myself to make sure I'm awake. Designing wardrobe for the Super bowl, designing outfits for Missy Elliott's comeback video W.T.F featuring Pharrell?! *All I can say is WOW-Thank you God.* I look at my circle of friends and family and I can truly see that I have everyone and everything I ever wanted-and ever needed. My mother is with me even more than I could ever imagine. I am surrounded by powerful and nurturing women who show me everyday-that giving up is not an option! I have amazing men in my life that completely make all past fears regarding men disappear. Love is no longer a fear.

The other day I was watching TV and saw something that made my heart smile with joy. I read the credits for The Wendy

Williams show- Talia Parkinson-Jones
Executive Producer. God is truly amazing! I
am so proud of all she has become. She
dreamt of it all-*don't know if she dreamt of
the Emmys?* Yes I said it! *Three-time
Emmy award winning* Television Producer
and Casting director! Tai from the student
office at HSTAT who said to me *I should join
the basketball team....* WOW! Talia was
now living her dreams as a Television
producer. And guess what.... She's going to
be a mom! She will be an amazing mother.
Life is truly amazing!

MY QUESTIONS ANSWERED

One day I was with Misa at her house with
her family and she was preparing to go to
Emily B and John Fabolous' baby shower in
midtown Manhattan that day. She invited
me to go. I immediately contacted my
childhood friend Paul Cain and asked if he

would be attending his brother's event. He said "for sure," so I decided to stop by to see him. At the baby shower, I saw a few of my friends there- Q hardy, Chrissy Lampkin, Mecca Moore, and Paul Cain. Towards the end of the night, I looked over at Misa to see if she was ready to leave. She was talking to an older woman who looked very familiar. I walked over and Misa introduced me. "Jai this is Mrs. Vicky, she knows your father." I was shocked! Mrs. Vicky knew my father? I sat down and we talked for a short while and she explained to me that she lived in Brevoort projects. Fabolous and Paul Cain's mother was Vicky's best friend. I was shocked and intrigued all at the same time.

Fate would have it that I would meet this wonderful woman named Mrs. Vicky. She lives in the 1853 Fulton Brevoort projects. Coincidentally, she lived in the building attached to my building. We decided to plan

JAI HUDSON

to meet so that she could tell me all she knew. And we did. I went back to Brevoort after 24 years of being away to talk to Mrs. Vicky. Misa drove me from Harlem to Brooklyn. It felt a little surreal. Crossing the Brooklyn Bridge, driving down Atlantic Ave, and pulling up to the housing complex I grew up in. I exited the car in front of 1865 Fulton and looked at the projects in awe. Misa smiled as if she knew I was about to embark on a wonderful experience. Everything looked so small but beautiful. I felt like a giant in an enchanted forest. I walked past my building and toward Mrs. Vicky's building. Everything looked the same, but the stores had been updated and there were endless trees planted outlining the buildings. I walked into Mrs. Vicky's building and got in the elevator. I felt so big inside of the same elevator that seemed so huge growing up. It

JAI HUDSON

still smelled the same too. Mrs. Vicky greeted me as I stepped off the elevator.

We sat and small-talked for a bit and then we got right into the mission at hand. What did she know about Ricky Washington, my father? She began to tell me that my father loved my mom and my father loved me so much. She recognized this a long time ago. All this time I never knew why my mom left him. If my father really loved us and if she loved him, then what happened? She confirmed that he did love us and she saw that my mom loved him. She told me that my father got sick and things began to change. Two years after I was born, my father began to suffer from schizophrenia. I knew he had this sickness, however I thought this happened to him after my mother left him. Now things started to make sense.

Mrs. Vicky told me that after my mom and dad broke up, he'd still come to Brevoort projects and sit in the playground, staring up at my window. She said he wanted to be where my mother and I were. He didn't know he was sick, he couldn't understand why he was losing his world.

I remember so strongly how whenever I looked into his eyes I immediately got a nervous feeling. I was afraid of those eyes. But I never knew why. Could I see his pain? Could I see what was happening to him? Memories of my father always start and end with his eyes. Drugs, lost love, abuse, life, his sickness; it all affected my father. My dad was only 25 years old when his world began to change.

I heard my mom and dad were inseparable in the beginning. Together every day. They did love each other and they loved me. Schizophrenia happened like an eclipse. The light overshadowed by the dark — an

JAI HUDSON

overcast. He didn't know that anything changed at all. But my mother did.

Imagine what it must have been like for my mom when things began to change. It wasn't something that she was prepared for. He went from being all that she loved — an amazing man with a great heart —and in the blink of an eye transformed into someone unrecognizable. The illness uncovered a person who became paranoid, dark, and scared.

My father gave me my face. There were things about me that I knew had a resemblance to him. That's part of the reason why I felt so different in my family. After recalling my past of experiences, a lot of questions I had are answered. I can now see that my mother fought hard to spare me emotional disappointments with my father. She got away from Ricky, but she ran into the arms of a monster. I endured sexual abuse from my stepfather and my mother didn't know how to get away this time. She was in too deep. Then there was so much dysfunction and sadness. And my mother knew what it felt like because she had experienced the same abuse. It broke her heart every time he came in my room. But she didn't know what to do.

When I think about my life as a whole, with all of the information, wisdom, and stories I now know and understand, I know that these were my set of challenges, my experiences to overcome. There was never a boogieman or scary faces — just experiences. Everyone has their own set of challenges and roadblocks. And they don't end until we leave this physical earth. We will keep experiencing. We will keep overcoming. That's just how life is.

However, we have the ability to change how the challenges affect us and how we perceive the experiences overall. I changed my perception. The situation I viewed as negative and painful became a chance to overcome. So my experiences started to change.

Have you ever heard the saying "What you think is reality?" I have deliberated on this phrase a number of times. I couldn't get past the idea that "what YOU think could be MY reality." Then I came to the conclusion that what it meant for me was, "What I think becomes MY reality." Yes! How we perceive a situation (think) becomes our reality (effect).

Mrs. Vicky and I walked into 1865 Fulton street in Brevoort projects on Tuesday May 26, 2015. We went up in the elevator to 5A. When we reached the 5th floor, in my mind, I could still smell Mama King's fried chicken lingering in the hallway. Every floor had their own smell back then. I walked down the

narrow hallway looking up at the ceiling that
was maybe a foot taller than I was. I ran my
fingers along the wall as I did when I was a
kid. I was directly in front of my old
apartment. This door held a part of my
childhood that had been a collage of
beautiful memories. This place shaped me. I
touched the door, put my ear to the door,
and paused for a moment. I used to listen as
a child to see who was in the kitchen before
going inside. I took a deep breath and
enjoyed the moment. Then I rang the bell. A
young woman in her early 20s opened the
door. She had a familiar face and familiar
eyes. She was very welcoming.

I walked through the door and looked to
my left at the kitchen where I'd run under the
table, scared of my daddy — or maybe I
wanted him to come find me. I looked over at
the kitchen window where Mama King
usually stood singing a country song, "I'm

talking, I'm walking..." repeated over and over and over. I had to laugh with joy in that moment. Oh how I wish I could hear that song again, sung in her Bajan accent. I looked back into the living room at the couch I thought I got eczema from. I hated that couch. Over the couch there used to be a picture of Jesus and the famous feast. I envisioned my table and chairs where I loved to have tea with my uncles and my mom. Wow…I turned back and started to walk down the hallway. The same hallway where I'd ride my red tricycle and scream "*beep-beep.*" I had so much fun as a child. When I reached my Uncle Pookie's room to the right, I looked in and could still see him lying on the bed, shirtless, and his withered security rag that had shrunken to a mere four inches in size, just sitting on his nose. It was a blanket from childhood that he kept even as a 37-year old adult. I wonder if there is a similarity to my scarf? Hmmm, maybe. Directly In front of me was Mama King's room. I saw her sitting on the bed, braiding her long silver hair before she went to sleep.

Then I turned left and walked over to the room that unlocked it all. I opened the door and saw a small room that I remembered to be huge with love. Crib to the right. Daybed to the left. I remember my uncle had stickers on the wall that spelled "GUN IT." He was referring to all the guns he possessed. However it also spelled out a major part of my future — 50 cent and G-UNIT. I looked out the window and looked directly across at the connecting building. Mrs. Vicky's window was facing my window. She lived on the same floor #5-it felt like I was looking in a distant mirror. *Everytime I looked out my window as a child, Mrs. Vicky was looking right back at me.* That was amazing to me. God's Grace!

JAI HUDSON

Wow, this small project apartment seemed like a huge penthouse apartment back then. Number 1865 was a building that held a treasure chest of memories for me. Brevoort was a community where I learned how to survive and learned the beauty in dreaming. I used to stare out my window from the 5th floor and see so many possibilities. I would try to envision being on stage like Michael Jackson. MJ had everyone's attention, and he sure had mine. I loved how that looked and felt from afar. You saw that people really loved him. I wanted to make people feel that way. When I saw a genuine care in someone's eyes, I wanted to keep creating that. My mother had that in her eyes for me, and for my father too.

Now I have found that feeling within me. I am the feeling. So the feeling I was longing for is right inside of me. Which means I can create that feeling whenever I need to. I am powerful. I am Love. I am Style. I am Truth. I am **Healed with Style and Grace**.

ANGEL 22

After my mom passed, I wanted to see her so badly. I wanted to know what she was feeling. I went to sleep every night hoping she would come visit me in a dream. On Easter morning of 2014, right before the sun rose, she came.

RESURRECTION DAY
Dream #1

I was walking down the hall in this beautiful house. The house looked like a mansion. It was as if I was walking through the halls searching for something or someone. I could feel the presence of my and sister but I never saw them. I walked past a room that caused me to back up and re-enter the doorway. I saw lots of sneakers placed on shelves. Every sneaker I admired and loved since I was a kid. I remember feeling like I didn't want to leave the room, but I also wanted to finish my journey. So I exited the room and continued walking through the house. At the end of the hallway there was a room that drew me to it. I went in and before my eyes I saw my mom in the fetal position laying on a makeshift bed. She got up out of the bed and started to do yoga positions next to the bed. It was if she was showing me that she now did yoga. I then remembered we had talks about doing yoga to help her legs. She then did a handstand on the bed to show me that her legs were working again. The whole time she never said a word. I remember trying to get her attention but it was as if she didn't hear me. Kind of like she didn't even know I was there. After that she went over by the bed and began to lie down again, but before she did, she said seven words that I will never forget. She said, "**Make sure you get out of there.**"

Dream #2- May 24, 2014

My mom, my sister, and I were in a room. My mother was folding some clothes near a dresser chest but seemed to be upset about something. She spoke as if she had no clue she had passed on. So I began to tell her what happened to her. She then arched her eyebrows, giving me her angry look. She said she had to do something for Leotta's birthday before she leaves. It was as if she knew she was leaving soon. However, It was my birthday just two days before, so I responded, "What about me? It's my birthday." She didn't acknowledge that it was my special day and that saddened me in the dream. My mom looked upset in this dream as she did in the previous dream. She did not smile. I wondered if I shouldn't have said anything about her passing. I woke up not feeling good at all.

Dream #3- December 2014

I was in a room and my mom came in. She didn't look sad like in the previous dreams. She actually looked happy. I went over to her and told her I missed her. She looked me in the eyes and told me she missed me too. I told her I was sorry. She sat down and gestured to me to lay my head in her lap. She ran her hands through my hair and touched my face as she did before all the bad dreams happened. I was so happy. Then I woke up.

I don't have dreams about her that often. I experience my mother in a spiritual way. I speak to her and ask her to respond by showing me the number 22. Twenty-two is the date of both of our birthdays. It's also the age my mom gave birth to me. I was also born at 11:22.

"22 is considered the most powerful of all the numbers. Those with a Life Path number 22 have great spiritual understanding, and ability to apply knowledge in a practical way and achieve enormous success.

"This is the number of the Master Builder and those with a 22 in their chart are able to turn dreams into reality. You are a great visionary and have the intuitive insights. Those following Life Path of 22 are called master teachers, and as mentioned they are the most powerful of the life path numbers, endowed with many powers, and a unique talent for manifesting ideas into the realm of reality.

"It's not easy to go through life thinking of yourself as a teacher. You are one, whether you like it or not. You will influence people just by being around them. You are not teaching behavior or something concrete. Teach peace of mind and contentment in the present. Teach by example."

That's so powerful. Maybe I'm going a little cuckoo by thinking she's responding. But I know my mother inside and out and I believe that for sure she's here with me. Maybe I couldn't handle the dreams, so by her connecting with me through our favorite number, she let's me know she's there like she has always been, but it's even more special now. I can feel her like I feel God. She's my angel.

I don't know why I'm here but I have reached the place where I excited about the unknown. I now know that the universe/God/Source is working with me and responding to my desires. The past is behind me. From this point on my story changes-the outcome can be whatever I want it to be, My past is only the ground of

which I stand on, a small part of the strength
accumulated which makes up my power. I
have Self-Love, I have forgiveness, I have
an Angel that appears as the number 22, I
have Optimism, I have Dreams, I have a
power in which I stand in and I have Grace.
I have it all and it all originates right inside of
me-Jai Hudson. I am me-Healed with Style
and Grace. PS I really really love you Jai ☺

"ENDLESS LOVE"

Song By Diana Ross And Lionel Richie

My Love
There's only you in my life
The only thing that's right
My first love
You're every breath that I take
You're every step I take
Cause I want to share all my love
With you
No one else will do
Your eyes they tell me how much you care
Oh yes you will always be
My endless love
Two hearts two hearts that beat as one
Our lives have just begun
Forever I'll hold you close in my heart
I cant resist your charms
And love I'll be a fool for you
I'm sure you know I don't mind
And yes you'll be the only one
No one can deny, this love I have inside
My endless love

AFTERWORD

By Jai Hudson

You can have all that you want. You can also feel exactly how you desire to feel. From the beginning of our life we are so often steered away from what and who we are. We are taught to admire others over self, taught to stay far away from emotions, told to develop a tough skin and work hard to survive by any means necessary. We aren't taught to love ourselves and we are definitely not shown how to do that simple task. I rarely heard growing up that forgiveness is key and that fears aren't real. Instead, I was taught that fear was real — from racism to being angry at anyone who has done me wrong, and that loving myself too much was being conceited and vain.

You can be free from the baggage that was most likely a part of you before you were even born. We can break the low self-esteem cycle. We have to develop our own set of beliefs. What do you feel? What do you believe? Times and things are always changing. Always know that you are never alone. We are all one and we all feel the same emotions —even though they are dressed differently. We have the ability to be better individuals for ourselves, for the sake of our children, and for the world.

Believe in yourself! God's creation! Uniquely made, a one-of-a-kind design! Claim your throne that Source has created for you! Own your set of cards called life and began to do the work on you! Claim your desires and believe in yourself so much that the process is empowering! I Love You and I champion you! That's Healing with Style and Grace!

MUSIC SOUNDTRACK

The music I used in the book will be used in the audio
book.
You can listen & download the Mixtape at:
www.Cre-8iveWorld.com

1. Intro- Notorious BIG- "Big Poppa"
2. Luther Vandross- "Amazing Love"
3. Big Daddy Kane- "Aint No Half Steppin"
4. MC Lyte- "Cha Cha Cha"
5. Mary J Blige – "My Life"
6. Whitney Houston- "If You Say My Eyes Are
Beautiful"
7. Salt-N-Pepa- "Expression"
8. Kirk Franklin -"Leon On Me"
9. TLC- "Waterfalls"
10. Lauryn Hill- "Tell Him"
11. Goapele- "Closer"
12. M.C. Lyte- "Georgie Porgie "
13. TLC-"Hat 2 Da Back"
14. Faith- "Faith" Interlude
15. The Roots & Erykah Badu- "You Got Me"
16. Total- "What About Us"
17. Puff Daddy & Family- "Victory"
18. Jay Z – "A Dream"
19. Notorious Big- "Sky's The Limit"
20. Jay Z & Alicia Keys- "Empire State Of Mind"
21. Teyana Taylor- "Sorry"
22. Mary J Blige- "Doubt"
23. Erykah Badu- "Bag Lady"
24. Michael Jackson- "Man in the Mirror"
25. Alicia Keys-"Diary"

JAI HUDSON

26. Fergie- "Big Girls Don't Cry"
27. Various Artists- "Freedom" Theme song from
Panther Movie
28. Faith Evans- (J-Cole Cover) "Be Free"
29. Monica- "Angel of Mine"
30. Tupac- "I Aint Mad At Cha"
31. Beyoncé- "Heaven"
32. Destiny Child- "Free"
33. Lauryn Hill – "Peace of Mind"
34. Missy & TLC – "Can You Hear Me"
35. Kanye West- "Good Life"
36. Missy & Aaliyah- "BestFriend"
37. Brandy-"Feels So Good"
38. Beyoncé-"I Was Here"
39. Mary J Blige- "Love is all we need"
40. Diana Ross & Lionel Richie- "Endless Love"

All lyrics provided by Google play,
www.metrolyrics.com
www.azlyrics.com

Thank you to all the writers who assisted me
with my journey of healing.

THE END.

JAI HUDSON

APPENDIX C
Love yourself — Put FOCUS back on YOU
BY Ajay Matharu

Your relationship with yourself defines your equation with others.

One of the most important relationships of all is the one you share with yourself. Unfortunately, most of us allow our perception of our own strengths and capabilities to be determined by those around us family, friends and colleagues. Their opinion is what we begin to believe as the truth despite the fact that we know exactly what heights we are capable of touching. And, as most of you in this kind of a situation will agree, it can often leave one with a sense of worthlessness as no matter what you do, you just never seem to meet anyone's expectations.

Love yourself

Most people say that if you love yourself,
you are a vain person. This, however, is far
from the truth. In reality, its more important
for a person to love themselves, even before
loving someone else. Its only when one is
comfortable with themselves and who they
are that you will be able to accept the other
person for who they are and love them
wholly, not because they conform to
your needs or wants.

The importance of loving yourself is very
significant because it helps one survive.
When you love yourself, you take pride in
yourself as an individual and attempt to
do your best in your chosen field of
endeavor. Positive self-love can be highly
motivating and encourage an individual to
achieve what they believe they can/should.
Self-love also propagates love towards
others because only when you
are happy with yourself will you do things,
not only for you but for others too. Loving
others is but an extension of loving yourself.
A mother who is not happy being a mother
can never love her baby. Similarly, if you
don't love yourself and you don't consider

JAI HUDSON

yourself worthy of love from others, you will be unable to spread your love to others. If we keep living by others opinions and expectations, we are doing great injustice to ourselves.

Each human was designed to be an individual and though society tries its utmost to tame our impulses, our individuality shines in some way or the other. Hence, those who accept their individuality and uniqueness are on a path of happiness while those who suppress it remain unhappy and miserable because they don't see a meaning to their lives. However, if loving oneself is carried to the extreme of narcissistic love, where it is only love yourself and give a damn about others, then the process of self harm starts. This leads to alienation and separation from others, which leads to isolation and unhappiness.

Believe in yourself

Though everyone may have their own opinion, remember that you and only you are the true judge of your capabilities. Each of us know our stretching point and our breaking point, and most often its much more that others will tell you. So no matter what happens, and how many times you fail, its only your belief in yourself that will give you the strength to get up, move on and cross that finishing line.

Ones motivation to achieve big things come mainly from believing in yourself and in your capability to do so. Apart from that, you also need to believe in your talents, values and the purpose of your task. Sometimes, the things people say may cause you to doubt yourself. But instead of losing faith and getting disheartened, it's better to look at the comments as constructive criticism. It is very important to nurture the ability to convert bad feedback into constructive criticism. At times, the quick pace at which your peers may achieve success can also be a de-motivator. However, it is important to remember that each person works at their own pace and that, just because you are slower, doesn't mean what you're doing is less good or less powerful that the other person.

JAI HUDSON

Forgive yourself

To err is human, to forgive divine.
Remember, this adage is as applicable to
yourself as it is to the other people around
you. Its very easy to chastise yourself
for mistakes made but you are just as
human and prone to mistakes are your
friends and close ones. Hence, just like
you'd forgive them for their mistakes, you
need to forgive yourself too. More than
anything else, it will give you that much
needed kick-start. Many people misconstrue
that forgiveness would make one more
callous and immoral. Quite the contrary!
Guilt serves zilch and the more guilty one
feels the more self-hating and that only
wastes energy and does nothing to improve
what needs to be improved. We are human,
and hence, mistake making and fallible. So
its only natural and human to err. The less
forgiving you are of yourself the more you try
and be superhuman a condition which is
impossible and unfulfillable. Forgiving
oneself doesn't mean
shedding responsibility for your actions, It
only means, giving yourself the right to be

JAI HUDSON

wrong, giving yourself the chance to be
imperfect! When you forgive yourself, you
give yourself a chance to correct, evolve and
grow as a person. When you forgive others
you do yourself a favor and are not
enveloped by feelings of hatred and
revenge. To err is human and not forgiving
isn't divine, it simply leaves you saner and
more realistic!
Thank You

Ajay

http://www.ajaymatharu.com/?s=love+yours
elf

Facts & helpful tips

You are Never Alone!
APPENDIX A

SEXUAL ABUSE OF CHILDREN AND ADOLESCENTS
By Tracy K. Cruise, PhD
Western Illinois University

According to data from the National Child Abuse and Neglect Data System, at least 12 of every 1,000 children in the United States were reported abused or neglected in 2001. More than 86,000 (9.6%) of the nearly 1 million children maltreated in 2001 experienced sexual abuse. Conservative estimates from incidence and prevalence studies suggest that 1 in 4 girls and one in 8–10 boys are sexually abused by the age of 18.

Suddenly these statistics may have a face and a name associated with them. Since children often experience more than one type of maltreatment, it is quite possible that several of these identified victims will also be victims of other abuse or neglect. Child sexual abuse can have immediate and long-term effects that span across an individual's physical, cognitive, interpersonal, and emotional functioning. Thus, it is important for parents and educators to familiarize themselves with the signs and symptoms of sexual abuse, know what to do if faced with a child who has been molested, and take appropriate steps toward the prevention of sexual Abuse characteristics. The federal definition of child maltreatment is included in the Child Abuse Prevention and Treatment Act (Public Law 104-235). Each state also has a criminal definition for sexual abuse that typically details age differences between the perpetrator and victim and is used to determine penalties. Although legal definitions vary from state to state, when sexual contact between a minor (someone under the age of 18) and someone 5 or more years older occurs, it is likely that the minor is being exploited.

Sexually abusive acts involve a child who is unable to give informed consent. There is an inequality of power between the child and the abuser on the basis of age, physical size, and/or the nature of the emotional relationship. Sexual abuse may take many forms and vary in terms of frequency, duration, invasiveness of the acts involved, and the use of force or coercion.

Examples of Sexual Abuse

• Tongue-kissing or kissing in a sexual way
• Fondling a child's intimate parts (breasts, buttocks, or genitals)
• Perpetrator rubbing intimate parts against a child's body or clothing
• Oral-genital or oral-breast contact
• Digital or object penetration (inserting fingers or objects into a child's anus or vagina)
• Intercourse
Non-Physical Acts
• Voyeurism or peeping
• Photographing the child's intimate parts
• Perpetrator exposing intimate parts

• Being forced to watch the perpetrator
engage in
self-stimulation
• Forcing the child to masturbate
• Forcing the child to view pornographic
material
• Making sexual comments to a child in
person, in writing, or by telephone

Abusers and Perpetrators

Contrary to the myth that most perpetrators
are strangers, children typically know and
trust their perpetrator. Males perpetrate the
majority (80–95%) of sexual abuse, though
there are certainly some cases in which
female offenders victimize male or female
children. Girls are more likely to be sexually
abused by someone within their family, such
as parent, stepparent, grandparent, uncle,
cousin, or sibling, while boys are more likely
to be sexually abused by someone outside
of the family, such as a coach, teacher,
neighbor, or babysitter. Adults, adolescents,
and even prepubescent children may
perpetrate sexual abuse.

JAI HUDSON

Unlike other forms of child maltreatment, sexual abuse by definition does not have to involve a parent or caregiver. The Internet is the newest medium that offenders have begun using to reach vulnerable children. A recent study surveying youths 10–17 years old found that 20% of those participants who regularly used the Internet (at least once a month) had received unwanted sexual solicitations and approaches in the last year. In some instances, the solicitor attempted to gain further access to the minor by phone, mail, or in-person meetings.

Potential victims

While there is no typical child victim, it is possible to make some assumptions about risk factors for being sexually abused. More girls than boys are sexually abused, although it is believed that boys are less likely to report their abuse than girls. Children who are emotionally needy because of family problems, poor parental supervision, and low self-esteem may be most vulnerable to sexual abuse because offenders deliberately target children who are responsive to their attention. Thus, force is frequently not needed. In some cases in which force, threats, or use of strength are involved, the offender is more commonly an adolescent.

Signs and Symptoms of Sexual Abuse

Sexual abuse often does not result in lasting physical injuries or produce clear observable evidence; however, it can be associated with various psychological and behavioral problems well into adulthood. There is no single child abuse syndrome or single response pattern for children who have been sexually abused. Factors that influence a child's response include age, severity and duration, invasiveness of the acts, relationship to the perpetrator, and the support and reactions from others. Some of the signs and symptoms of sexual abuse may seem subtle and less likely to be related to sexual abuse.

The following symptoms are indicators of possible abuse (Gil, 1991; see "Resources" at the end). The psychological and behavioral responses listed are not unique to victims of child maltreatment, but might also be indicative of Attention Deficit Hyperactivity Disorder, Oppositional Defiant Disorder, or Bipolar Mood Disorders. Parents and educators should use these indicators to prompt them to consider the possibility that a child has been sexually abused and remain open to additional confirming or disconfirming information. Sensitive parents and educators can pick up important clues by observing children, remembering that it is often a cluster of indicators or history of symptom presentation that make up an abuse composite. Some of the immediate and long-term consequences a child might experience as a result of being sexually abused include:

Health and Physical Consequences

• Pregnancy, especially in early adolescence
• Sexually transmitted diseases
• Difficulty walking, sitting, or standing
• Torn, stained, or bloody underclothing
• Vaginal/penile discharge

• Pain during urination or urinary tract
infections
• Bruises on the child's mouth, to the hard or
soft palate
• Sleep disturbances (difficulty sleeping,
nightmares)
• Self-injurious behavior (cutting, burning
oneself, suicide attempts)
Cognitive Development and Academic
Achievement
• Age-inappropriate sexual knowledge
• Sexually explicit drawings (not open to
interpretation)
• Sudden changes in academic performance
• Refusal to participate in certain activities
(dressing
for gym)
• Difficulty concentrating
Emotional, Psychosocial, and Behavioral
Development
• Sexualized play (frequent sexual themes
with toys or other children)

**Sexual Abuse of Children and
Adolescents
Helping Children at Home and School II:**

JAI HUDSON

• Frequent touching of genitals or masturbation
• Inappropriate sexual expression with adults (frequent hugging of a female teacher that produces arousal)
• Aggressive sexual behavior with use of force or verbal threats
• Socially isolated or withdrawn
• Extreme fear reactions
• Dependent or clingy behavior
• Poor social skills
• Substance abuse or delinquency, especially in adolescents
• Difficulty trusting others
• Fire setting
• Cruelty to animals
• Running away

What to Do if a Child Makes a Disclosure

The most reliable indicator of sexual abuse is a child's self-disclosure.

• Offer a supportive and nonjudgmental response. Make sure the child knows you are listening and taking the matter seriously. Try not to overreact emotionally because this may cause the child to end his or her story or recant what has just been offered.

• Assure the child that he or she did the right thing in telling you.

• Tell the child he or she is not to blame for the abuse.

• Inform the child of what you will need to do with the information (make a report to child protective services or the police) and give the child some idea of what to expect (for example, the child may be interviewed by a social worker or police officer, and you will check in with the child the next day).

• Make an abuse report. All educators are mandated reporters of suspected child abuse and neglect. Although not mandated in all states, parents are also strongly encouraged to report reasonable suspicions of child abuse.

Supporting Sexually Abused Children

• Provide a safe, healthy recovery
environment at home and school.
Remember the involvement of at least one
caring significant adult in the life of the child
victim is an essential ingredient for positive
outcomes.

• Provide firm clear limits to help children feel
safe. A child who has been abused may
perceive a lack of control in his or her
environment so limits that are clear and
consistent will help the child feel more
secure and regain a sense of personal
control.

• Be respectful of personal boundaries. A
trusted adult has already harmed the child's
body so it is imperative that others in the
child's life be sensitive to issues of personal
space and touching. A simple hand to the
shoulder may trigger a strong emotional
response from an abused child.

• Be aware of community resources and help
the child and/or family find appropriate
services. Some services may be offered at
school or at a local agency.

JAI HUDSON

• Remember that each child may respond differently to abuse and may need different responses from adults. Children who have been abused should be treated as individuals with a wide range of characteristics and needs influencing their response and recovery. Remember, change takes time.

Suggestions for Parents of an Abused Child

• Take your child for a medical examination, preferably to a pediatrician who has experience with sexually victimized children. This exam may lead to the collection of evidence (such as bodily fluids or fibers) but will also test for sexually transmitted diseases and pregnancy.

• Acknowledge your own thoughts and feelings regarding the abuse (such as guilt, anger, sadness, inadequacy). Recognize that if you were maltreated as a child, you may experience flashbacks, a flooding of emotions associated with your own trauma, or anxiety or depression that may influence your response to your child and also your parenting in general.

• Seek individual (for child and/or self) or family counseling if needed. Again, you should try to find a specialist in the area of child sexual abuse or trauma.

• Continue to try to balance self-care and childcare. Maybe more than before, your child may need for you to be calm and emotionally capable of interacting with him or her. The practice of self-care will also demonstrate to your child how to deal with his or her own emotions or distress.

Preventing Sexual Abuse

• Know the signs and symptoms of sexual abuse so that you might recognize a child who is being harmed.

• Be willing to report suspicions. Remember, it is not your job to prove that sexual abuse has occurred, and your report might keep a child from further harm.

• Offer ongoing communication about sexual touching and other topics to create trusting relationships with children.

• Teach children self-protection skills that they have
the right to say no or stop and to tell an adult and
keep telling the adult until they are believed.

• Support community and school programs to prevent abuse. Abuse induced alienation.

Stage 4: Emerging Adulthood
Child abuse induced suicide.

Knowledge:

To prevent suicide in emerging adulthood-help a child or adolescent if you suspect that he or she is suffering from child abuse, neglect, any maltreatment.

Primary prevention of suicide due to child
abuse must occur in childhood.

Primary prevention of suicide due to child
abuse recognizes the role of the abuser in
causing the suicide.
Because really, when you get down to the
facts of child abuse induced suicide, the
cause of death is the abuser

The abuser is the cause of death.

JAI HUDSON

APPENDIX E

RESOURCES

You may find it helpful to contact local physicians, mental health centers, and human services agencies.

FOR TEACHERS

Civitas. (2002). Right on course: **How trauma and maltreatment impact children in the classroom, and how you can help.** Chicago, IL: Author. Available: www.civitas.org

Gil, E. (1991). **The healing power of play: Working with abused children.** New York: Guilford. ISBN: 0898624673.

Horton, C. B., & Cruise, T. K. (2001). **Child abuse and neglect: The school's response.** New York: Guilford. ISBN: 1572306734.

Monteleone, J. A. (1998). **A parent's and teachers**

handbook on identifying and preventing
child abuse: Warning signs every parent and
teacher should know.
St. Louis, MO: G.W. Medical Publishing. ISBN:
1878060279.

Seryak, J. M. (1997).
Dear teacher, if you only knew...:
Adults recovering from child sexual abuse
speak to
educators.
Bath, OH: The Dear Teacher Project.
ISBN: 0965942112.

Tower, C. C. (1992).
The role of educators in the
prevention and treatment of child abuse and
neglect.
Washington, DC: U.S. Department of Health and
Human Services, Administration on Children,
Youth, and Families.

U.S. Department of Health and Human Services,
Administration on Children, Youth, and Families.
(2003). Child maltreatment 2001. Washington,
DC:
Author.

JAI HUDSON

FOR PARENTS

Adams, C., & Fay, J. (1992).
Helping your child recover from sexual abuse.
Seattle, WA: University of
Washington Press. ISBN: 0295968060.

Hagans, K. B., & Case, J. (1988).
When your child has been molested: A parent's guide to healing and recovery.
San Francisco: Jossey-Bass. ISBN:
0787940739.

Kleven, S. (1998).
The right touch: A read-aloud story to help prevent child sexual abuse.
Bellevue, WA:
Illumination Arts. ISBN: 0935699104.

FOR CHILDREN AND ADOLESCENTS

Allen, S., & Dlugokinski, E. (1992).
Ben's secret.
Raleigh, NC: Feelings Factory. ISBN:
1882801008.

Bean, B., & Bennett, S. (1997). **The me nobody knows: A guide for teen survivors.** San Francisco: Jossey-Bass. ISBN: 0787939609.

Girard, L. W., & Pate, R. (1992). **My body is private.** Morton Grove, IL: Albert Whitman. ISBN: 0807553190.

Kehoe, P. (1987). **Something happened and I'm scared to tell: A book for young victims of abuse.** Seattle, WA: Parenting Press. ISBN: 0943990289.

Mather, C. L., & Debye, K. E. (1994). **How long does it hurt? A guide to recovering from incest and sexual abuse for teenagers, their friends, and their families.** San Francisco: Jossey-Bass. ISBN: 1555426743.
Websites

National Association of School Psychologists. (2004)
Sexual Abuse of Children and Adolescents. Bethesda, MD

JAI HUDSON

Nicola Fernandes
Energy Coach & Shaman
Time Line Therapy® & Hypnosis Master
Practitioner
phone 917-208 8188
www.coachingshaman.com
www.BecomingAHealer.com

Misa Hylton
Life Coaching & 360 Transformation
Life Coach
www.MisaHylton.com
www.MisaHyltonFashionAcademy.com
@MisaHylton

REFERENCES

Bureau of Justice Statistics. (2011). Sexual Assault.
(Data is from the National Crime Victimization Survey and does not include data on victims 12 and younger.) Retrieved from:
http://www.bjs.gov/index.cfm?ty=tp&tid=317
Peter. (2008) Recovery from sexual abuse, rape and molestation. Self Empowerment and development center. Retrieved from:
http://www.iempowerself.com/50_sexual_abuse_molestation.html

https://www.nsopw.gov/en/Education/FactsStatis tics?AspxAutoDetectCookieSupport=1#sexualab use

Caruso, Kevin. Rape Victims Prone to Suicide. Retrieved from: http://www.suicide.org/rape-victims-prone-to-suicide.html

Chaffey, Lisa; Unsworth, Carolyn A.; Fossey, Elle. (2012).
Relationship Between Intuition and Emotional Intelligence in Occupational Therapists in Mental Health Practice. Retrieved from:

http://ajot.aota.org/article.aspx?articleid=185154
5&resultClick=1

Cruise, Tracey K. Sexual Abuse of Children and
Adolescent

Dillard, Sherrie. (2010). Your Intuitive Connection
to Love. The Llewellyn Journal. Retrieved from:
http://www.llewellyn.com/journal/article/2118

Eby, Douglas. Creative Expression and Sexual
Abuse. (2014) Retrieved from:
http://blogs.psychcentral.com/creative-
mind/2014/01/creative-expression-and-sexual-
abuse/

Einstein, Albert. (2015). A letter from Albert
Einstein to his daughter: about The Universal
Force, which is LOVE. Retrieved from:
https://wearelightbeings.wordpress.com/2015/04
/15/a-letter-from-albert-einstein-to-his-daughter-
about-the-universal-force-which-is-love/

Hall, Karyn PhD. (2012). A Few of the Many
Ways to Distort Reality. Pieces of Mind.
Retrieved from:

https://www.psychologytoday.com/blog/pieces-mind/201208/few-the-many-ways-we-distort-reality

Matharu, Ajay. (2010). Love Yourself: Put the Focus Back on You. Retrieved from: http://www.ajaymatharu.com/?s=love+yourself

Myers, Seth PsyD. (2012). The Wives of Pedophiles Always knows the truth. Retrieved from:
http://www.psychologytoday.com/blog/insight-is-2020/201206/the-wives-pedophiles-always-know-the-truth-0

Meyers, Seth PsyD.. (2012). The Wives of Pedophiles Always Know the Truth. Insight is 20/20. Retrieved from:
http://www.psychologytoday.com/blog/insight-is-2020/201206/the-wives-pedophiles-always-know-the-truth-0

National Association of School Psychologists. (2004)
Sexual Abuse of Children and Adolescents. Bethesda, MD

National Institute Mental Health. What is
Schizophrenia? Retrieved from:
http://www.nimh.nih.gov/health/topics/schizophre
nia/index.shtml

Nauert, Rick PhD. (2008). Suicide Risk Among
Abused Children. Retrieved from:
http://psychcentral.com/news/2008/08/04/suicide
-risk-among-abused-children/2685.html

Prescott, Gregg M.S.. (2015). Introverts and
Spirituality. Retrieved from:
http://in5d.com/introverts-and-
spirituality/#sthash.mCE5yPm3.WfTJ3tlm.dpbs

Psychology Today. All About Fear. (2014).
Retrieved from:
https://www.psychologytoday.com/basics/fear

She Knows Media. Meaning of Jai. Retrieved
from:
http://www.sheknows.com/baby-names/name/jai

Tanner, Jennifer L. PhD.. (2011). Suicide at Age
27: Death Due to Child Abuse. Psychology
Today. Retrieved from:
https://www.psychologytoday.com/blog/becomin
g-adult/201101/suicide-age-27-death-due-child-
abuse

JAI HUDSON

Tracy K. Cruise, PhD. (2004). Sexual Abuse Of
Children And Adolescents. Western Illinois
University. Retrieved from:
http://www.nasponline.org/educators/sexualabus
e.pdf

US Department of Justice; (2012). Facts and
Statistics Sexual Abuse. Retrieved from:
https://www.nsopw.gov/en/Education/FactsStatis
tics?AspxAutoDetectCookieSupport=1#sexualab
use

US Department of Justice Raising Awareness
about Sexual Abuse Facts and Statistics

Wikipedia. Child Sexual Abuse. Retrieved from:
http://en.wikipedia.org/wiki/Child_sexual_abuse#
Psychological_effects

Wikipedia. US Department of Justice Raising
Awareness about Sexual Abuse Facts and
Statistics. Retrieved from:
http://en.wikipedia.org/wiki/Child_sexual_abuse#
Psychological_effects

All music lyrics were provided by Google Music,
www.azlyrics.com, www.metrolyrics.com

AUTHORS PAGE

The point where style meets music and creativity meets vision is the place you can find Jai Hudson. Born in Brooklyn NY's BedStuy, Jai was raised in the 80s where being out of the box was celebrated. Motivated by creativity, she knew early on she had major artistic talent.

Jai became a Celebrity fashion stylist groomed by celebrity fashion stylist Misa Hylton at Chyna Doll Enterprises, providing image consulting and wardrobe for some of music's top recording artist and television personalities.

Early on, Jai recognized her knack for developing upcoming artist and providing much needed artist development. After working for 7 years as a stylist she realized her niche was developing new talent. She secured a recording contract for Teyana Taylor with Startrak/ Interscope and produced the MTV my super sweet 16 show for Taylor, which became the most watched

MTV sweet 16 to date.

Where this industry thrives off of established artists, Jai loves to develop new talent from the beginning stages and provide the elements needed to establish the careers of budding talent.

Jai has worked at Angela and Vanessa Simmons' Pastry line, helping to brand the sneaker company as a "cool" sneaker for the teenage demographics. In 2012 Jai partnered with Misa Hylton by creating and opening a Fashion Styling academy in New York City, the Misa Hylton Fashion Academy. Where they provide the knowledge necessary for young fashion stylists to have a successful career in the business.

Jai Hudson's expertise is in marketing, creative development, product management has become her strengths in this industry. However, Jai loves to stay amongst the young generation recognizing early on that the children are truly our future.

JAI HUDSON

Jai now embarks on a new area of creativity through this literary work. Her passion to be heard is the driving force behind the creation of this book. She is already working on her follow up to Healed with Style & Grace- dealing with abuse from a male perspective. Jai is very passionate to address those uncomfortable situations in a creative way.

Follow Jai Hudson @JaiHudson_
Facebook: JaiHudson
Twitter: JaiHudson
www.cre8ive-world.com

Made in the USA
Las Vegas, NV
24 March 2022

46231078R00295